The Pottery Gardener

The Pottery Gardener

FLOWERS AND HENS AT THE EMMA BRIDGEWATER FACTORY

Written and photographed by
Arthur Parkinson

For Sheila Parkinson and Minnie Florence Brown

First published 2018

The History Press
The Mill, Brimscombe Port
Stroud, Gloucestershire, GL5 2QG
www.thehistorypress.co.uk

British Library Cataloguing in Publication Data.
A catalogue record for this book is available from the British Library.

ISBN 978 0 7509 8557 4

Typesetting and origination by The History Press
Printed in Turkey

Frontispiece: Me and Christopher, my Buff Cochin cockerel. (Photographed by Matthew Rice)
Above: Me in the greenhouse inspecting a crop of dahlia 'Totally Tangerine' before moving them down to the garden.

Contents

Foreword

When Arthur blew into Stoke-on-Trent to take in hand the neglected garden hidden away in our factory it was a happy day.

Despite his youthfulness, he brought huge botanical knowledge and a depth of understanding about how to put on a show in a garden – and to make his appointment a pleasure, he brought charm and a winning empathy with the brand of Emma Bridgewater. Most importantly of all, he demonstrated a great enthusiasm to make a real go of the challenge.

He has created a marvellous result: from early spring through to late autumn the factory garden is a rare and wonderful oasis – all the more thrilling because of its context in a rather beaten-up, grey cityscape.

The waves of colour rush in and out of the walled enclosure with frequent explosions as surprising as firework displays as his skilled planting scheme evolves, but I'm constantly fascinated by the fact that there is never an off day – and I know just about enough of gardening to recognise this is no small achievement.

The book's loving photographs amply demonstrate his conviction that gardens must be personal, colourful, refreshing and inspiring. He supplies bountiful information about all his favourite annuals and a chapter on keeping chickens – truly no gardener could fail to draw some delicious new treats from this banquet of enthusiasm.

From all of this, you can understand that Arthur is unusual, with an idiosyncratic style – both botanical and literary – all of his own. I am completely charmed by him, by his infectious and generous enthusiasm, as well as his energy and staying power. I especially love his writing about his mother and grandmother; these two admirable women clearly laid down a remarkable early education for him. And Arthur has gone on to seek out other interesting women to enrich and inform his journey, and to learn all he can from them; this book is a disarming tribute, firstly to the Duchess of Devonshire, and next and probably most influentially to Sarah Raven, whose vast talent has clearly cast a deep and magical spell over Arthur. I should also mention Matthew Rice as a big influence on him, though I'm happy to say that Arthur set his own rigorous standards for order and cleanliness in the henhouse!

This book is bursting with ideas and facts, with love and dedication – I recommend it from my heart.

(And personally, I am making a resolution to look for more dresses with prints inspired by feathers!)

Emma Bridgewater, January 2018

The tulip 'La Belle Epoque', with petals of smoky pink washed with hot chocolate froth brown. This colouration has seen it become one of the most in vogue of tulip varieties.

Introduction

Behind a red-bricked wall and along a busy, long road is one small, unexpected garden – a young garden, made up of raised flower beds, galvanised dustbins, cattle troughs, a hen house and broody coops and supported by two rooftop greenhouses, which are high up and out of view. The garden is set in what must be one of the most industrial urban places you could imagine.

Venetian-coloured blooms, a buzzing of bees and the hurried strut of hens are to be found here, surprisingly in great profusion. All of this life and rich beauty is accessed via a little corridor attached to a shop filled with mugs, plates, bowls and tea towels. These all lovingly display fowl and flowers on them. How unique, to have their real-life influences growing and clucking just metres away from the shelves on which they sit.

This book is about the walled garden located at the working British pottery that is the Emma Bridgewater Factory in Stoke-on-Trent and how I came to be its gardener.

Crested miniature Appleyard ducklings. At just a day old their beaks still show the sharp egg tooth that has helped them hatch; it will shortly fall off having now served its vital life-emerging purpose.

Me, picking tulips.

PART ONE

The Gardener

High summer in the courtyard. Cosmos 'Rubenza', flowering bronze fennel and nepeta 'Six Hills Giant' spilling over the raised beds sleepers and being airy and light enough in habit to resist damage during windy days.

Persian carpet
wallflowers scattered on
an Emma Bridgewater
wallflower plate,
giving real scent to the
hand-sponged tributes.
The plate is on an equally
rich floral tapestry.

Mill Yard

I come from a world of small, urban gardens. My mother's garden is the front yard of a sandstone cottage nestled in the middle of the once greenbelt-edged, ex-mining town that is Hucknall, part of Nottinghamshire's sprawling city outskirts. Mill Yard's garden is little more than a bricked-over square of land that separates the mallard-drake-green front door of the house from its neighbouring road. There is no room for a shed or greenhouse here, just brick, stone and some precious soil.

The garden fork and spade are cleaned off outside with a hand brush after their use, and they are stored with the hoover and broom – leaning together in a corner of the kitchen. Seedlings and summer bulbs are grown on the (thankfully generously sized) window sills. The small porch over the front door acts as a largely unreliable, yet still worthy, cold frame.

My mum has always grown flowers. The spicy, rich scent hanging in the air on still days from the flowering carpets of wallflowers in April are an annual spring reminder of my early childhood. Mum would often collect me and my brother from school holding blue plastic bags containing bunches of these bare-root biennials. Their clay-clagged bottoms would be wrapped in newspaper, having been bought en route from Hucknall's Friday town market.

Mum's little cottage was festooned with beautiful things, and indeed still is. Chests of drawers and trunks are covered with découpage, the snippings of photos from gardening and antiques magazines. The bathroom walls were once covered with mermaids, parrots and cherubs cut out from beautiful wrapping paper prints bought from those delightful shops that my mum refers to as 'full of things that would be totally useless in the event of a nuclear bomb'.

Me and mum would garden together when I was little and I'd also, on occasions, help my Grandmar Sheila with flower arranging, but I didn't really have a huge longing to do either endlessly then. The horrid feeling of a dry oasis seems like yesterday and has put me off the disgusting green blocks for life – a vase is surely much better.

Along with my younger brother Lyndon, who, as a fat, adorable curly headed tot, would assist mum with the carrying of shopping home from the local Safeway supermarket in his plastic pedal-on tractor (this had a handy little trailer on the back of it), I have been lucky to have a close relationship

Looking down from my bedroom window, Mill Yard in late April. The garden is little more than the size of stamp. Forget-me-nots self-seed with relish in the mortar around the bricks. Dolly tubs, galvanised urns and large terracotta pots enable this space to become an overflowing mass of colour and excitement through the seasons.

with both of our grandmothers – Sheila, our mum's mum, and Min, our dad's mum.

Minnie Brown has a long vegetable garden that was once full of potatoes, runner beans and leeks. At 91, she has now had to stubbornly release much of it to 'the wildlife'. Vegetables stir little excitement within me, I prefer to eat with my eyes, but I do like cabbages as winter bedding plants – herbs too; rosemary (*Rosmarinus officinalis*) and sage (*Salvia officinalis*) provide much-needed foliage in the winter months.

On warm days, Nannar Min can be found dozing outside her back door. Often, on her outside table, there will be a cup and saucer of lukewarm tea and beside it an old spray bottle. The bottle in question is so old that the sun has bleached its once bright-yellow plastic to that of a spent chewing-gum white. On its side is a hardly visible scribble of writing, written by Nannar, which only she can read. I'll ask her, just for fun (knowing the answer), what the spray bottle contains while watching the nozzle slowly prepare to drip a drop into her cup of tea below – 'A bit of bug killer for the black fly.'

While I did appreciate the colours of the flowers that my mum grew at home, between flowers and fowl it is the hens that came first in my life. As a toddler, I immediately became intrigued by the clucking of hens that could be heard through the hedges of the local allotments during walks to nursery. A glimpse of a hen could sometimes be seen through the old hawthorn hedges, which would be thick with the clacking of the blackbirds within them. Hedges act as urban rainforests, and these lined the decades-old, trodden earth pathways of the allotments around the old pit mines of Hucknall.

One allotment plot was kept by friends of Grandmar Sheila and Grandad Ted – John and Gillian. John had a greenhouse that he had made out of many different glass window panes, and best of all he had a coop full of brown hens from whom he would let me collect the eggs. The freshly laid, warm eggs of the hens were to be found in straw-filled old fruit boxes.

There are a few precious sites from my mum's pram-pushing days still in cultivation today. Dear John and Gillian have long since passed, but their allotment is thankfully still in existence, albeit there are no hens kept on it now. Their plot is lucky – so many across the country, indeed thousands of plots all with their own tales and characters who once tendered to them, have now fallen under the shadow of new-build housing. And alas the hedges too.

Above: Me aged 5 with John's allotment hens. These were brown hybrid girls, known locally as warrens. Fresh chicken droppings are acidic and quickly kill grass roots, resulting in bare ground. The seasonal use of garden lime will help stop the ground from becoming stale.

Above right: Minnie Florence Brown, my Nannar, in her garden. The youngest of nine children, she became her father's favourite within the family pecking order due to her watering his roses and chrysanthemums each evening.

It was during the school summer holidays, spent in Derbyshire's Peak District, that I could truly indulge my growing passion for chickens that had seemingly come from nowhere – no one in my family kept them, or knew much about them. Being a greenbelt brat, these holidays with Grandmar Shelia and Grandad Ted were a time of forming an enduring love of the countryside. We stayed on a working farm that offered camping and caravan holidays, near Matlock.

Without this, my life wouldn't have featured farming in it at all. My pre-school education, looking back in terms of its awareness of life's modern elements, was a disgrace. The most shameful aspect of it was perhaps a school trip where the whole class were taken off to McDonald's and shown around the 'restaurant', without a mention of a cow as we all happily munched down our burgers with glee. Afterwards, we spent a day designing our own restaurant (still no mention from the teacher as to where any of the food for it was going to come from) and the following day, when we were taken to the local library, I was told off for venturing off into the adults' section to seek out books on smallholdings rather than the advised reading of *Ronald*

McDonald's Fairy-Story Farm, where no animal has to be killed to become part of a cardboard-enclosed 'happy meal'. Secondary school food technology classes were no better either – a potato pie required a sachet of Smash, which my mother thankfully refused to buy.

Holidays in Derbyshire on a real working farm thankfully ensured exposure to things beyond tarmac, greed, labels and childhood obesity, and so our minds received an injection of much-needed reality that wasn't provided at school. Fortunately for us, the late nineties were before the time of over-the-top health and safety legislation – the sort of risks usually mentioned today by those in suits standing in suspiciously clean boots. It was a *Darling Buds of May* era for us, staying on the farm as its guests and allowing the place to continue as it always had – a true, working farm with all the daily life, death, muck and smells that went with it. Now such places have had to become much more urbanely sterilised to please countless inspections and, indeed, the modern expectations of today's clientele. More and more, alas, we are becoming a society that seems to be afraid of good dirt.

Mill Yard tulips: T. 'Antraciet', T. 'Orange Favourite', T. 'Abu Hassan', T. 'Black Hero'. Rich, berry and cardinal tones for me will always reign supreme. The occasional flash of salmon and candy-cane pink can be excused, but the tones of white and pale yellow have to be totally barred as they are not complementary to the richer tones.

Dawn in Derbyshire, Grandmar Sheila at the walking club. Today my grandmother is president of Hucknall's flower club and takes great comfort from the small garden that surrounds her bungalow. (Ted Parkinson)

On the farm, we would stay in a hut, known fondly as the 'walking club bungalow'. It was a simple, wooden building with electricity, running water, bunk beds and little else. Evenings were spent talking and playing games. It was called the 'walking club' as it was rented out to a club of Derbyshire ramblers, and Grandmar and Grandad were some of its most enthusiastic members, knowing the paths of the Peaks like it was their own back yard.

A huge, old, caramel-bodied cow would wander down from the farmyard, waking us up with her mooing at the door each morning. The blue skies would be full of screaming swifts, skimming in a macabre, swirling ballet for midges. I will never forget the feeling of the damp, dew-hugging Derbyshire grass clinging to my feet in the mornings and sunny days consisting of picnics, paddling, bully head fishing and endless walking.

Hens of the Duchess

The treat of the week's holiday was, for me, a visit to Chatsworth House, the aptly named 'Palace of the Peaks'. Jumping out of the car within the shadow of this grand yet beautiful house, I would soon be surrounded by dozens of hens jostling about. They knew that, like many visitors, we had brought a picnic that contained sandwiches and they had learnt that children, especially, were more inclined than adults to share such tasty offerings with them.

Hens are comforting, charming creatures, underestimated in their character by those who haven't kept them. They are animated, poised and seemingly happy in their activities. If you watch a few hens pecking and scratching about in the dry soil of a hedgerow bottom, then you are surely seeing the true meaning of contentment.

The hens of the Chatsworth car park were a hundred-plus flock of mostly red-brick and puddle-brown hybrid ladies. These Heinz 57 sorts would lay their socks off until they die. They were sharply diluted by white-feathered, highly strung and quick-footed American white leghorns with bright red combs that flopped over to one side of their faces. Pretty, golden-necked, plump, shy Holland Welsummers, which lay beautiful, rich terracotta-coloured eggs (albeit far more sparingly in numbers than their previously mentioned hen-house sisters), were the most stylish members of the flock. Mighty, wallflower-orange-necked and mahogany-bodied Welsummer cockerels broke up this all-female party into harems of several dozen, with each male taking charge of his ladies and touring them around the parked cars each day in separate tribes. At the discovery of picnic crumbs, they would summon their many wives and mistresses at once with excitable clucking.

The chickens all roosted and laid their eggs in a great hexagonal, grey building that sits magnificently with the Cavendish family's snake crest carved above its doors. Today, this former game larder-turned-hen house is empty of hens, but has now been restored and is sitting in its own little hollow on the edge of the car park as it has always done. When the hens were in residence, their sawdust litter hid a swirling mosaic beneath their perches.

My Grandad Ted, noticing my constant ventures off to this great hen house, found me peering through its pop-hole squares (the entrances specifically made for hens to enter and leave their hen houses, not for small boys to peer through, to the alarm of the sitting birds inside). He told me that the hens

Her Grace Deborah Duchess of Devonshire holding one of her Buff Cochin cockerels in the shadow of Chatsworth House. The Cochins were the only birds to be allowed free-ranging rights in the Chatsworth gardens while the other breeds were kept penned. This privilege was due to the Cochins having steady natures, which saw them being able to cope with the summer crowds. The duchess saw much success in the showing of her Cochin chickens, exhibiting at poultry shows throughout the country. This included the now sadly no longer Royal Show and the still in existence National Poultry Show. (By kind permission of Bridget Flemming)

belonged to the Duchess of Devonshire, and so I wrote a letter, addressed to Chatsworth, telling Her Grace how much I loved seeing her chickens and about the two hens that I was allowed to keep at the top of my Nannar Min's vegetable garden. A postcard from Ireland showing an ivy-clad Lismore Castle arrived a week later, and so began more than a decade of yearly correspondence between myself and Deborah Devonshire about our mutual adoration of hens.

'Debo' (as she was known to all who knew her) kept hens within the garden at Chatsworth, as well as in the car park and at large in the farmyard and adventure playground, long before it became an in-vogue pursuit. Today, a hen run seems to be the must-have finishing touch to any potager-styled plot, and seemingly every pet shop has a specific aisle now for poultry sundries.

Like myself, Debo's passion for chickens began in early childhood and carried on throughout her life. While known to most as the youngest of the famed Mitford sisters, one of her most enduring passions was the keeping of hens, and she did so with the greatest of style as the 11th Duchess of Devonshire. This style I picked up on as a child.

The chicken drinkers in Debo's hen runs would be of strong and visually pleasing galvanised zinc, always scrubbed clean, free from algae and placed on breeze blocks to help keep out the dirt from the birds' scratching. The hen houses' pop-holes always showed clean shavings to be found within them and the runs (if they were absent of grass) would have ground that was covered with a mud barrier of good, sweet-smelling wood chippings. In the summer, the farmyard would have a row of triangular wooden arks that held broody hens with their chicks. The families would be seen pecking about on fresh grass. The dates they had hatched and what the various breeds of the multi-coloured little chicks were would be written on each of the run doors, which enclosed the proud mothers and their broods. At the factory, I am constantly repainting signs on the hen house and broody coops telling visitors who is in residence.

All the Mitford sisters had been exposed to hens as young girls, as their mother, Lady Redesdale, kept Rhode Island Reds and Light Sussex for their eggs. The sale of these eggs paid for the girls' various governesses. It was, however, most noticeably Deborah and her sister Pamela (who was known for her countrywoman lifestyle) who inherited their mother's passion for chickens the most.

Top: Postcards sent to me from Deborah Devonshire. Chicken mugs by Eden pottery and Catriona Hall, bought from Chatsworth by me after months of saving up pocket money. Such merchandise, which reflected the hens, garden and farmyard, were chosen personally by Debo as shop stock for Chatsworth during her reign as Duchess of Devonshire. Several postcards carried images of her chickens, one included a hen looking up at Chatsworth's famous 'Water for dogs' sign, which influenced me to write the same title on a painted slate by the factory's café doors.

Left: The highlight of summer: feeding the hens of the duchess. (Ted Parkinson)

Pamela was responsible for the first importation of the flighty, crested and Dalmatian-like plumed Appenzeller Spitzhauben chickens into England. After asking the permission of the agricultural minister several times to import some birds from their native Switzerland with no response, Pamela took matters into her own hands and brought over clutches of fertilised Appenzeller eggs to hatch on British soil. The kitchen garden, today one of the most beautiful attractions of Chatsworth's great garden, was once a grassy slope and was an idea of Pamela's; Debo especially liked the excitement of having edible herbs and veg amongst the flowers.

Debo once took a goat on a train during the war and had to milk her during the journey to Mull in the first-class waiting area of Stirling Station. I haven't much of a fondness for goats (complete garden wreckers!) but I have carried hens with me on trains. Cochins and Orpingtons, which are quiet and don't flap, can be trusted to be allowed to poke their heads up from an open box on a train seat, calmly peck from an offered hand of mixed seeds and then sip a drink from the cap of a water bottle – they don't seem to be at all fazed. Some of the hens at the bottom of Sarah's vegetable garden have experienced trains and London Underground services before arriving at Perch Hill!

My first hens, brown Warrens like Debo's beloved car park girls, were kept at Nannar Mins. They lived in an ark made from oak that my dad had built for me. This hen ark was sturdy and solid and took a huge effort to move each week in order to provide the hens with fresh grass; the lawn suffered hugely, but the ark stood firm against the fox and rot.

After they had ravaged Nannar's purple sprouting broccoli for a season, they returned to their original home to make way for more softly mannered bantams. Their original home was a smallholding that belonged to Anne and Tony Whyte. It was on Anne's kitchen dresser that I first saw Emma Bridgewater pottery, although at the time I had no idea what it was or any interest in it. Anne collected Matthew's songbird mugs and I do remember the mass of them – depicting pheasants, blue tits and thrushes, to name but a few – crammed into a hulk of an oak dresser.

Being a talented carpenter, my father has made me many hen houses over the years. When the time came for more young hens to be sought, always ones of rare breeds and in even rarer feather colours, Dad would take me to various shows and breeders, often waiting in the car at Chatsworth as

Barbie girl spring: tulip 'Chato', fooling those who gaze upon her into thinking that she is a peony, arranged with cherry blossom in the shop.

Above: A Silver Partridge Pekin bantam hen with her chick (of uncertain lineage) amongst several Emma Bridgewater hens on nests and pure-breed hen mugs.

Left: Tulip 'Blue Parrot' with nepeta 'Six Hills Giant', a nectar-rich perennial which will flower from the middle of May and again in late summer if cut back to its base in June. It's a good plant to pair with lavender in well-draining soil as it blooms in between the lavender's midsummer flowering.

I returned excitably with a box of new, young blood for the coops at home. The hens that travelled in his Volvo have enjoyed listening to the tracks of Bob Dylan while they sat motionless in their boxes wondering what on earth was happening to them.

The Gift of a Mug

When I left secondary school, my dad urged me to consider studying some form of trade. The only one of appeal to me was gardening, and so I did a year's RHS course at Nottingham Trent University's rural branch at Brackenhurst College, near Southwell Minister.

The year went by fast, thanks largely to an Edina Monsoon-like lecturer called Caroline. I discovered that I had decently 'green fingers' and I enjoyed the hours of work under glass, sowing seeds and growing the resulting plants. As the end of the course drew near, I knew that I needed more gardening experience and so, on something of a whim, I applied to be a trainee at Kew Gardens, in London. After an interview that saw me unable to utter more than a handful of Latin names and wearing a shirt that drowned me, I was, to my great surprise, offered a year's paid training.

Suddenly, I was living in London, studying in the hardy display section of the great, yet unfamiliar, pedigree of Kew Gardens. I was without my hens and therefore without the therapeutic rituals that poultry keeping entails – dawn feeding, the twisting off of metal drinker tops, the letting out, evening egg collecting and shutting the hens in for the night.

On one visit to London, my mum produced a present for me, it was a mug depicting a lavender Pekin Bantam hen. I loved it, and so I began collecting them. Curious about the mug's origins, I discovered the story of Emma Bridgewater, and along the way I discovered that it was her husband, Matthew, who drew and painted the hen mugs, while Emma focused on sponge designs. At this realisation, and having read that he also kept poultry, I penned Matthew a letter thanking him for his hen portraits on the mugs that reminded me so much of my longed-for fowl. With me now being 19, Matthew's reply was via email. 'Dear feather brained Arthur, perhaps you are unwell and should seek immediate medical attention?' was the opening line …

Discovering Sarah and Finding the Gardener

As I filled my tiny bedsit with Emma Bridgewater mugs, and emails on the subject of chickens pinged back and forth between me and Mr Rice, I also began visiting the garden that is, for me, the perfect model of what a human-made collection of plants should be – Perch Hill. This Eden, nestled in the rolling farmland of East Sussex, has been grown by my gardening idol, Sarah Raven.

I met Sarah on the bank of her greenhouse on one of her garden open days. She was picking salad while surrounded by a flock of ladies, and I suppose I was a different sort of visitor to the norm. Once I got over being star-struck, a friendship formed.

That morning, I had set off from London Charing Cross Station into unknown territory. I disembarked the train at Stonegate Station, which has

The Oast Garden, Perch Hill, in early spring. Tulips: T. 'Brown Sugar', T. 'Ballerina', T. 'Sarah Raven', T. 'Jan Reus'. Long tom terracotta pots are placed along the seemingly naturally occurring pea shingle path, and are planted differently each summer after the tulips fade with beautiful but always unusual and bright summer bedding such as salvias, nasturtiums and dahlias. The garden is the benchmark of what a lavish and jungle-like garden should be: free, lush, dramatic, yet somehow also managed so it doesn't feel messy.

a platform as near to the one out of the *Railway Children* as you could hope to find in the modern world – long, often quiet and very leafy, but booming with birdsong. From here I set off on my Google Maps™-researched walk of 4.5 miles to Perch Hill. A long, winding, grass-lined road edged up and down until finally the drive of Perch Hill came into view.

A cockerel crowed as I walked through the hazel sweet pea avenues. The garden was purer and more beautiful than I could have imagined. It was large, yet modest, not overly grand, but still hugely exciting and striking. It wasn't trying to battle its way through the natural chemistry of its surroundings; indeed, it was totally blended into the rolling hills with its surround of hawthorn hedges. It felt as if you had fallen down a rabbit hole and entered a productive and honest Eden, where the plants were free enough to have their own voices.

On one open day as the visitors left, I sat down with Sarah in the barn and she kindly offered me a summer of working at Perch Hill, once I had finished my studies at Kew. While Sarah and her husband Adam were away for a few weeks, I had their dogs Curly and Frizzy to look after, but it was rather them looking after me. I had not been brought up with dogs, so it was a learning curve. Luckily Tessa Bishop, who manages the courses and office at Perch Hill and has taught me much in the world of floristry, came to my rescue on many occasions.

Mornings were spent carrying Frizzy – who is more of a koala bear suffering from on-and-off dementia than a dog – to spare his ears being chewed by Curly, who at that time was an excitable labradoodle (plus collie) puppy. Each morning, we marched across dewy fields, disturbing pheasant poults seeking sanctuary, before we returned home for breakfast – or, rather, they had breakfast, as I can't stomach much until the late afternoon.

After a year of London nightlife, where light pollution was at its worst, the sheer blackness of the East Sussex sky at night was as if one was a budgie whose owner had covered the cage over with a black sheet – totally engulfing, a jet-black tar-like sky, broken up only by stars and the twinkling fairy lights that had been festooned over a vase of cut artichokes in the greenhouse. The fairy lights, being solar powered, would come on as soon as they sensed the grip of night taking over from the last rays of sun. Within minutes the whole place would be in darkness and I would be chasing after Frizzy as he suddenly came alive, barking and running after the hoots of owls.

Sarah's books carried me through my horticultural studies. These decadent, beautiful bibles are never far from my bedside, and continue to be close companions to this day. At Mill Yard, in the year before I left to study at Kew, Sarah's book, *The Bold and Brilliant Garden*, had completely eclipsed my mind. I'd save up any spare money that I had earned through part-time work and buy tulips from Sarah's mail order company. I planted them into dolly tubs, packing them in and waiting longingly for their mass flowering, either side of the front door, come April. April is, to me, when the gardening year truly starts and the dank of winter is moulted off properly. So I invest in the garden flowering at its most exuberant for this month onwards, rather than in the colder ones before it. The late species narcissi give way to the tulips, whose flowering signals the true arrival of the sun.

I quickly developed a very definite personal idea of what I felt a garden should be; they should be jazzed-up rainforests, not spaces where human influences are harshly visible. I didn't want to see bare soil, fence panels or have plants growing in rows. I was instantly drawn to certain plants. I liked the tall, engulfing ones, with huge leaves and flowers in sultry colours that commanded attention and that appeared as if they could burst into colourful

Perch Hill, late September. The Spanish flag climber has succeeded the early summer sweet peas, which fade out by August, ensuring a continued late summer show, wrapping themselves up the central cutting garden arches. Certain plants do better in southern gardens rather than northern ones; these, along with zinnias and Mexican sunflowers, sulk in the factory garden – cosmos, thankfully, thrive.

conversation if you looked at them for too long; but at the same time, I loved the English cottage border too.

In terms of colour, I like the deep pinks and reds as seen in the feathers of ruffled flamingos, the orange flesh of ripe mangos, the rich, excitable lime yellow of the frogspawn-like insides of passion fruits, the deep blues of peacock necks and coffee-froth browns, but never the white or pastel shades of nursery or care home walls.

I began to appreciate foliage as well as flowers, because leaves give flowers a supporting cast, backing them up and making them all the more beautiful. I like thugs in the garden too – willow herb, teasels and buddleia can all be assets if kept in careful check.

Just because a space is small, it doesn't mean that the plants have to be. Indeed, matching small spaces with small plants can only make them feel more modest within their frames. Instead, it is surely better to feel as if you have stepped into a lavish, rich world where fronds and petals dominate.

I want my hens to be part of a garden space too, not kept constantly behind chicken wire. By now, I had kept many breeds of chickens and I had discovered that varieties such as Pekin Bantams and huge Cochins were ideal as garden birds. I quickly became averse – a snob – to the hanging basket, and to anything dinky or plastic. I like the large and aged, in terms of containers and garden props – old dolly tubs, troughs, metal coal-house buckets and leaking, unusable galvanised chicken drinkers.

At Mill Yard, my mum had amassed many beautiful vases and bottles. I began to pick the flowers from the garden and place them singularly and simply into them. In doing this, the garden and cottage were suddenly connected to one other, married in the most organic, visual form of, albeit fleeting, pure, unrivalled beauty.

Emma Bridgewater

I had never visited Stoke-on-Trent before and an internet search of 'the garden at the Emma Bridgewater Factory' resulted in hardly anything substantial, in photographic or written content, to reveal what I was heading to. Matthew, in one of his emails, had asked me to go and visit, having spoken

Above: My first summer at the factory, a summer show totally reliant upon annuals that included quick-to-flower seed-grown cornflowers and the dahlia 'Bishop's Children'.

Below: Me, content, picking annual cornflowers in my first summer at the factory.

about me with Sarah – they thought it might be worth my while visiting to see what I thought of the garden.

When I first visited, it was on a rather depressingly grey February day. The dirty-sink-cloth sky spat down sleet as I walked, unsure of my exact direction, from the railway station to the factory. Upon my arrival in the garden, pushing open a reluctant fire door that connected it to the gift shop, I was met with a blank canvas of earth and gravel, and a collection of variously past-it and broken office furniture. I stood in its centre and surveyed this little walled space that was surrounded by the human world of bricks and mortar.

My first work within the garden was carried out on this visit. I pruned the dormant apple trees that had been planted in the middle of the garden's two central flower beds. The movement of my feet on the raised beds caused a fat worm to rise to the surface. I smiled – I knew that this space, which had once been used as a factory dump and was now turned into a garden created through Matthew's vision, was something very special and could, within a few months, be a canvas of colour and beauty and portray a zest for life. It would complement the sponge work and illustrated flowers and hens found on the

An Oxfordshire Sandy and Black piglet with its mug visiting the site during Farmyard at the Factory, an event where a local farmer – in this case from Park Hill Farm – brings his pigs and sheep. They, together with the resident chickens, turn the courtyard into a true if alas temporary farmyard, and visitors see at first hand the native rare breeds that inspire the drawings on Emma Bridgewater mugs.

pottery being made and sold just a few feet away. This element of connecting beautiful ceramics to their real-life inspirational forms was one of the job's biggest and most unique appeals.

Having said yes to the job, my first spring as gardener was something of an embarrassing, bare-earthed affair, with me having not been in the garden the previous autumn to plant spring-flowering bulbs. Just two rows of precious tulips provided the only colour to be seen until the spring-sown annuals began to flower. Learning just how many plants needed to be grown was a sharp learning curve in that first season, with cosmos now requiring to be grown in the hundreds. Perennials are slowly taking hold to ease this need, but these grow at a slower pace than the quick-to-flower annuals. The days of late April see me trundling back and forth through the factory with a trolley from the rooftop greenhouses containing seedlings on their way to their final planting places in the garden.

The walled garden has now expanded into the factory's main courtyard. Two huge raised beds sit there now, like great beached whales, containing many tons of soil. All the flower beds at the factory are raised because the original canvas that they sit on is not earth but brick, cobble and concrete. The fight between earth and concrete has been further supported with the introduction of galvanised bins and cattle troughs, planted up seasonally to create an oasis of colour that directly greets the factory shop and café visitors, while the walled garden acts as a final surprise to all who venture through the shop and its corridor, leading to a welcome of flowers and various poultry.

What began as a want for colour and beauty in my life, I now see as a crusade of backdoor conservation through the growing of nectar-rich flowers. The bee and butterfly have both been left starved and threatened by intensive agriculture, urbanisation, pesticides, herbicides and the cultivation of largely pollen- and nectar-absent modern bedding plants that are still used en masse by most councils today. It is up to the gardener, in my view – all of us who have some outdoor space, no matter how tiny it may be – to provide a sanctuary to these crucial insects that form the basis of our planet's food chains.

Almost all of the flowering plants written about in this book are bee and butterfly attractive, and while the factory garden is wildlife friendly, it isn't messy (at least I hope it isn't), it's just that the flowers, in the main, have beckoning, open centres that are full of nectar. Despite the factory garden

being in the city, on a sunny summer's day it is abuzz with bees coming and going all day long. I now get as much pleasure from seeing a bee on a flower that I've grown as I do from cutting the flowers from the garden to arrange.

While beautiful chaos is (in my mind) the look that is always wanted – a combination of William Morris and Henri Rousseau – it has to be controlled and, indeed, managed. It is managed with concealed staking, feeding, deadheading and weeding, which is needed throughout the year.

Succession of flowers is something that is learnt and perfected year upon year too, requiring the taking of notes and photos to look back on, come the winter, to help you know what went well and what needs more thought. There are hard times for a small garden, and a small space is less forgiving if there is a lack of flowering ooze, most notably in late May and early June, when the dance of the wallflower and tulip has long since turned sour and the glitter-ball purple of the *Allium* has begun to fade to its seed-head green. My solution? A fortnight-old brood of surprisingly dependent, late-April-hatched call ducklings, waddling with confidence about the garden as if they are on parade down a London pavement. Their activities will soon distract

any visiting eyes away from freshly planted annuals and dahlias still putting down their roots before beginning to bloom! If you cannot take to rearing ducklings, then an easier answer is June-flowering foxgloves (*Digitalis*), but if you can, nurture both.

If you are without a greenhouse, then you may have to buy in a few seedlings, simply due to not having enough windowsill space to grow everything that you desire, but with mail-order nurseries selling a wider range of seedling annuals than ever before, there has never been an easier time to grow what you like.

What I didn't want this book to be was a heavy thing with tons of text. Elements of it, I hope, may prove to be of some practical use, but having myself amassed (like most gardeners) several shelves worth of books on the subject, I can divide them into two piles. One is of those that are for visual, inspirational use, much needed in the winter, and the other is for those that are practical and informative, often with very few pictures. This book is aimed at being in the first mentioned pile.

Above left: Slate that I often gather out of skips is used as signage to great effect.

Above: The view of the garden's back wall from Lichfield Street – the factory's main entrance.

Right: Tulip 'Ballerina' in a polka bowl once made for an event involving porridge, now it sits on the roof near a staircase window.

CAFE

Emma
Bridgewater
Since 1985

FACTORY
SHOP

Cosmos in the courtyard.

The view of the garden from the shop corridor. Here a brahma hen is wearing a saddle – a piece of stiff fabric to protect her from the cockerel's passionate attentions.

Jute pea netting makes
a good, yet attractive,
poultry barrier.

Tulips in the courtyard. The Darwin hybrids are joined by mid-season tulips such as 'Ronaldo' and 'Brown Sugar'.

Clockwise from top left: The life of the pear 'Conference'.

PART TWO

The Emma Bridgewater Garden

The beautiful moss rose 'William Lobb', more a flower from a cloud forest than a cottage garden, They are just reaching the top of the wall at the time of writing.

Walls

Matthew planted several pears against the walls of the walled garden that have been trained in an espaliered fashion. They are of the varieties 'Beurre Hardy' and 'Conference', and both help to cover the garden's walls and high trellis. They have to be pruned in the summer, with each spur rising upwards from the main tree's skeletal outstretched arms needing to be taken back to three buds – a technique I have yet to fully master, since it seems too dominant and controlling for me to warm to.

The pear blossom in the spring is divine and as pure in its form as any flower could hope to be. The fruiting of the pears later in the year sees visitors appear out into the garden from the factory's inner sanctum who only seem to visit at this time of year!

Tough *Sleeping Beauty* roses and blackberries are being planted up the walls too; these will then act as natural security against any foes, once their spine-eclipsed growth has matured.

Raised Beds and Soil

There is no surface of the factory that you could dig a spade into. For flower beds to be born into such an environment, where the natural soil has long since been suffocated by concrete and cobbles, they must be created upwards rather than downwards, in the form of raised flower beds. There are now two large ones in the main courtyard, along with those that have formed the garden behind the gift shop since Matthew visualised the space as a garden. The soil is contained within the beds by thick, treated wooden sleepers that are painted black on all sides, with a thick, protecting tar-like paint that will keep the damp of the soil from causing them to rot from the inside out. The raised flower beds cannot be simply built on top of a hard, concreted surface, however, as they could on bare earth. To do so would be like creating an upper storey of soil that would dry out within days, like a hard brick.

Firstly, the concrete where the flower bed is going to sit has to be cracked open and the resulting rubble dug out and down to a good few inches, to ensure that the bed drains well. For large flower beds, the help of a mini digger

Buff Cochins in the main factory alleyway.

Above: Raised bed being dug out in the courtyard.

Above right: Courtyard tulips. The first to bloom are the large and perennial in habit Darwin hybrid 'Gentle Giants'.

Left: The raised bed along the café wall in mid-June with a display of alliums and foxgloves.

proves invaluable and makes short work of this part of the build. Once this work has been done, the painted wooden sleepers can be pieced together like a game of Jenga®, drilled and fixed to one another. With the sleepers secured, the empty beds need to be filled with the miracle, life-giving substance that is soil. The raised beds eat soil by the ton, which is not surprising if you consider the amount of soil needed to fill just a large garden container.

Soil is the beginning of everything for a garden, and it needs to be looked after. When you dig into good, healthy soils they are rich, like moist chocolate cake, full of living goodness and wiggling with worms. Some gardeners mulch their flower beds each spring to enrich their soils and help them to look prim and proper, ready for the growing season ahead. Rather than do this (as mulches prevent self-seeders such as Shirley poppies (*Papaver rhoeas*), I add fresh compost and manure to the soil when I'm planting any new plants into it and I just mulch closely (but thickly) around the bases of hungry plants such as roses, rather than applying it to the entire flower bed.

Good top soil is required as the main filling for raised flower beds. The top soil is mixed towards the top surface of the bed with compost and trusted

Above: High summer – a cluster of bins creates a central jungle in the walled garden with salvia 'Macrophylla', cosmos, dahlias and gladioli.

Opposite top: Blossom, narcissi 'Geranium' and tulips – an urn has been placed within a flower bed to give extra height.

Far left: In my first summer, cosmos were planted in pockets of broken concrete along the café's wall. Here the building of the first courtyard bed is beginning.

Left: Work in progress.

farmyard manure that is not full of weed seedlings – horse manure is the worst of the lot for containing these! Manure that contains earthworms is especially useful, as the introduction of worms into new flower beds will help ensure a good soil chemistry because they have the positive effect of increasing levels of good bacteria and fungi in the soil.

Raised flower beds are a good system to use, on the whole. They reduce having to bend down and, as the factory garden proves, they allow beds to be formed in spaces where they otherwise couldn't be created. Their downside is that they dry out, sometimes surprisingly fast in the summer, which is why ensuring that the beds have good drainage and that their soil chemistry is of the highest quality is vital for them to be successful areas of raised gardening for all times of the year.

Tulip fortnight – pots
of tulips planted in
lasagnes have been
placed within the flower
beds to give easy pops
of colour. Tulip varieties
include 'Sarah Raven',
'Antraciet', 'Ballerina',
'Brazil', 'Arjuna' and the
species tulip *T. whittallii*.

Dustbins

I love containers within a garden. For some of us this is all a garden can be and, in some ways, you could argue that the entire factory garden is container gardening on a grand scale. For the factory garden, the trick was finding something that matched the factory's industrial look.

At Mill Yard, dolly tubs line the path to the front door, having been rescued from abandoned allotments by my mum after they had been left to rot amongst waist-high nettles. These vintage old dears now command a high price at reclamation yards. In a corner of the factory garden, when I arrived, were two metal dustbins full of rotten corn. I emptied and washed them, then stood back and admired them – suddenly there was something solid amongst the vastness of the gravel (there were no other containers). Most importantly they looked immediately at home, giving presence and matching the factory surroundings – not looking too posh, twee or out of place. Soon a dozen more were ordered from the local hardware merchant.

The bins arrive sparkling silver and fresh, but within a year they weather up nicely, turning a preferable aged grey. Before filling each bin with compost, I turn them upside down and then drill several holes into the base. The holes are essential so that water doesn't sit in the bin's base. Good drainage is necessary for all containers as soggy soil leads to the rotting of bulbs over the winter. Once their bases are drilled, I fill the base of the bins with a deep layer (about 15in) of crocks to further aid the drainage of water. Broken bowls, plates and mugs are in no short supply at the factory, but broken terracotta, roof tiles, gravel and even broken polystyrene all make good materials to use as drainage in containers.

After the crocks, in goes the compost – by the bagful. The bins eat compost up and each takes a full 70-litre bag of multipurpose, then another few extra spadefuls. If I have it, I'll mix well-rotted manure into the compost too, as I'm filling the bins, so that the compost has an immediate extra additive of nutrients, just as it does when filling the larger raised beds.

Plants in containers, especially varieties like dahlias or those in summer displays, need more feeding and watering than those in the ground. Organic chicken manure pellets are what I feed the summer containers with. These pellets are solid when you buy them. I soak them overnight in a large bucket and then once they have turned to a soup, I'll add more water to the bucket

Dahlia 'Totally Tangerine' and fronds of millet growing in the planted dustbins at full pelt in August. The bins are placed in rows for visual impact; each bin backs up the ones before and in front of it with bursts of colour.

Above left: Dustbin in the green. Wallflowers and Cerinthe major in February.

Left: Dustbin with tulip 'Queen of the Night'; wallflowers 'Sunset Purple' and 'Sunset Pink' and alliums are emerging too.

Above: A dustbin replanted for summer. The tulips have been removed but the *Allium christophii* remains, with a summer consort of dahlia 'Totally Tangerine', salvia 'Amistad' and red millet planted around them for a show that will bulk up quickly as summer progresses.

Right: Tulips 'Chato' and 'Brown Sugar' with wallflowers. The central bin has been planted with sweet peas.

and pour the brown liquid full of goodness into the watering can to water everything with it. The whole process is a smelly business but it is one that ensures lush, healthy foliage and profuse flowering. For autumn planting of bulbs, handfuls of bone meal can be mixed into the soil when they are being planted, as their energy is stored within them. Spring displays need far less feeding than those of the summer, though.

Troughs

While the introduction of the dustbins to the garden was a success, I felt that too many of them looked a little like an army of *Doctor Who* Daleks about the place! I found the answer one winter when coming across some old cattle troughs at my friend Julian's farm and discovering that they were due to be collected by the scrap metal man. They instead arrived at the factory a few weeks later to begin a new life as planters to diffuse the shapes of the dustbins.

They were placed either side of the gift shop door, lifted up a little by cobbles on each of their corners. They give a very solid presence and look good either standing as islands or filling up a whole corner of a garden. The process of making them fit for life as containers is the same one that the dustbins go through. I have ordered more troughs in as new galvanised ones since the original used trio arrived. The cost of these new, considering their size and compared to that of a long tom terracotta pot, is good value and they will give a long and useful life to any garden space.

Please note: it is important to place them in their definite final resting places before filling them with soil – once they are full, moving them is almost impossible without a forklift!

Above: Form of the garden upon concrete troughs. Tulips: T. 'Jan Reus', T. 'Orange Favourite'.

Right: Tulip table trough – 'Sarah Raven', 'Whittallii', 'Brown Sugar', 'Ballerina' – with alliums in bud.

Trough Pond

Water in a garden gives it another dimension – of reflection and relaxation. I'm not a fan of hearing splashing, flowing water all the time, so the idea of fountains and cascades does not appeal to me, but the tranquillity and wildlife that just a small, still area of water provides certainly does.

A trough that has been kept for its original purpose (holding water) sits in the middle of the walled garden. It is surrounded by a hazel and willow picket fence to stop any children from getting their hands wet! A number of aquatic plants, marginals, submerged oxygenators and regal waterlilies are grown within it. Their roots act as the best natural filter system and are vital for keeping the water clear and sweet. It is topped up with collected rainwater to keep its chemistry fresh.

While container ponds (unless they are dug into the ground, as a traditional pond would be) don't allow access to crawling toads and the majority of modestly jumping frogs, they can still provide water for birds to drink and bathe in, and to bees that need to drink each day too. (Bees will even transport water back to the hive to help it stay cool in the heat of summer.)

Above: *Thunbergia* climbing over the birch pond cage, softening it as it comes into bloom, having been planted in a pot against the troughs walls to grow across it for the summer.

Left: Waterlily 'James Brydon' flowers are especially sensitive to the sun, only opening in its rays, and each bloom lasts just a few days before closing forever. Despite being the most divine of all flowers they are seemingly almost forgotten by many gardeners.

Greenhouses on the Factory Roof

My offices are on top of the factory's back roof, and they are two greenhouses. Matthew put them here having realised that the excess heat that the roof was releasing due to the pottery kilns being below it would make this flat expanse of roof the perfect, secure place for the greenhouses to be.

For my style of gardening, which involves sowing seeds and taking cuttings almost over the whole year, the greenhouses are always full, with plants endlessly going down to the factory garden having started life on the factory roof. It is a constant turnover of plants, and all this propagation requires constant attention.

In the spring, the kiln heat proves to be very helpful, but by midsummer (when foxgloves and wallflower seedlings are starting life) things can become too hot and this can cause problems for germinating seeds – umbrellas are often the answer! The expanse of the factory roof is totally flat so the rainwater stands on its black surface, quickly creating large lakes of about an inch deep. With the heat of the sun and kilns, these lakes begin to steam

Above left: Seedling shade for wallflowers and foxgloves growing in July.

Above right: The greenhouses surrounded by water after a heavy shower; good boots are required to wade through the temporary shallows.

Left: The greenhouse crammed with potted dahlias, salvias, cuttings and annuals in mid-May ready to go down into the garden for summer display. Bright watering cans ensure that they are easily spotted amongst the foliage. A turnover of plants within the greenhouse and keeping things clean and organised helps to naturally keep pests at bay.

Right: In the winter the hens move into the greenhouse, their droppings helping to fertilise the beds for growing tomatoes in. They enjoy the best rays of the winter sun here too, sunbathing and scratching while being protected from the wind and rain. However, good ventilation for them in essential.

as they evaporate, creating a scene fit for an African soda lake. The puddles attract insects that, in turn, attract tail-bobbing grey wagtails with their bright lemon bellies. They appear almost always in pairs, flitting along the puddle edges and snatching seemingly invisible bugs from the water's brown scum.

Staking in the Garden

A large number of the lush summer plants are not exactly self-supporting, and to give the garden another vertical dimension, wigwams and arches make the space seem far bigger and allow for a whole array of climbing plants to be grown, such as the favourite sweet peas.

Bamboo canes are not natural things to have in a flower border, being too clean and sleek-looking for me. I want my plant supports to show good structure in the spring as they await their use, while the plants they will bear are either being grown in the greenhouse or awaking below them in the ground. Once these plants are growing at full pelt, I want the stakes to disappear as background supporting artists for the A-list show-stopping performers.

Each winter, I go out onto derelict land around the factory and cut down self-sown silver birch seedlings. These young whips make the perfect material to weave into thick nest-like supports or for bunching together to create wigwams. Unlike willow, their stems when pushed into the ground won't root in the garden. For climbers, the twig-like nature of the birch is adored by their touch-sensitive tendrils and stems, which wrap around them within hours compared to the unwelcoming smooth, slippery surface of a bamboo cane.

To create a silver birch nest, take three to five young but thickly stemmed whips of birch, all of a similar length, and push them into the ground surrounding the crown of a tall growing perennial, such as a delphinium, in March. Turn each whip into a tight plait and then bend each of them slowly downwards so that the supporting nest will be about a foot above the ground. Weave them together and encircle the plant until the last two whips meet and then tightly weave these so that the nest is secure. If it still feels floppy or not tight, add more stems of birch to weave into the nest.

For garden arches, the straight and thick branches of hazel are useful, but hazel doesn't grow as freely as silver birch does, so this comes from a

Top: Sweetcorn sprouting.

Far left: Seeds of sweetcorn 'Popcorn Fiesta'.

Left: Strawberry corn cob. These last forever once dried and look beautiful, especially over the autumn and winter, scattered in bowls and when used in wreathes.

Above: Grid supports.

Opposite top: A summer storm rips through the garden, this is when staking proves invaluable to save plants from becoming ruined within moments.

Far left: Supports of silver birch await their use, having been woven over the winter, while wallflowers give some good green presence during the cold months.

Left: Silver birch nest above growing gladioli at Perch Hill.

local coppiced woodland supplier. Huge amounts of woodland used to be traditionally managed as hazel coppices, and this management of woodland is very good for wildlife. The light that coppicing creates reaches the woodland floor, encouraging wildflowers and creatures such as dormice. Coppiced hazels also live a much longer and more profuse life than those that are left to grow to their own devices. Using the hazel branches as a straight, upright arch or as tunnel supports hammered firmly into the soil, the more pliable silver birch can be bent between the uprights to create a curved roof for a sweet pea tunnel. The arches and tunnels are tightly tied together with hessian string. If you're using very thick branches, use a handheld drill.

For large areas of the garden that are given over to plants such as dahlias, which without doubt need staking, a noughts-and-crosses grid of hazel is created after they are planted out in the spring. Several thick posts of hazel or birch are hammered into the ground, then longer, slimmer branches are tied between them and across one another, both vertically and horizontally. The dahlias then grow up through the branches and are well supported. A timesaving recent creation, copying this method but making the whole job far quicker, is the use of jute netting, which is brown twine produced in a mesh-like form. The netting is spread over an area, ensuring that it is taut and held in place using thick posts of hazel. As before, it is placed above plants such as dahlias and cosmos to grow through it. I stake the beds in the main factory's courtyard using this, as it can be especially windy.

A lot of people are fearful of gathering silver birch in case they are told off or harm the trees. If gathered correctly, it can have a positive effect to the young wild saplings, as they will become bushy and better looking adult trees! Do seek permission from the landowner and gather the birch responsibly, leaving healthy plants by cutting branches cleanly down to the tree's main stem and at angles. Only gather material during the winter months when the trees are dormant.

Succession of Planting

My gardening year is split into three: mid-spring, when the garden properly opens; early summer to late summer; and then to Halloween.

In essence, when I look at the garden, I see youth (spring) and middle age (summer) almost sliding into the pensioner era (autumn), and this is alright, but what I never want to look at is death. However, death is part of a garden – after all it's all alive. To beat death means giving the garden a constant injection of youth with plants that have been forced a few weeks earlier than they otherwise would be in the greenhouses. As a result, for example, I'll get *Dahlia hortensis* 'Totally Tangerine' joining *Allium christophii* for Literary Festival week. The alliums will have been left in the dustbins while the fading tulips around them will have been removed to make room for the dahlias. It's a task of constantly slotting things in and out. The trick to make things easier is to ensure a backbone of perennials that you know will help ease the numbers of annuals needing to be sown each spring, to allow some self-seeding of good thugs and self-supporters, and to plant a good layer of plants for foliage.

Opposite right: Bantam hens pecking about the path under the birch tunnel as the sweet peas begin to climb with gusto. There is also flowering kale 'Red bore' and Chard.

Right: Wigwam of *Thunbergia alata*; they will bloom cheerfully until a hard frost.

Far right: Building work.

WE ARE BUILDING ANOTHER BIG RAISED AB-FAB FLOWER BED!

Cosmos and millet avenue – high summer in the walled garden.

Weeding the cobbles –
Silver Laced Wyandotte
Bantams in a factory
alleyway.

Mid March.

Sweet peas in full bloom.

Ducks in June.

Mid-May late tulips. The purple and lilac wax-like 'Victoria's Secret' and 'Blue Parrot' are accompanied by alliums 'Purple Sensation' and the yellow of a flowering row of kale in a neighbouring bed.

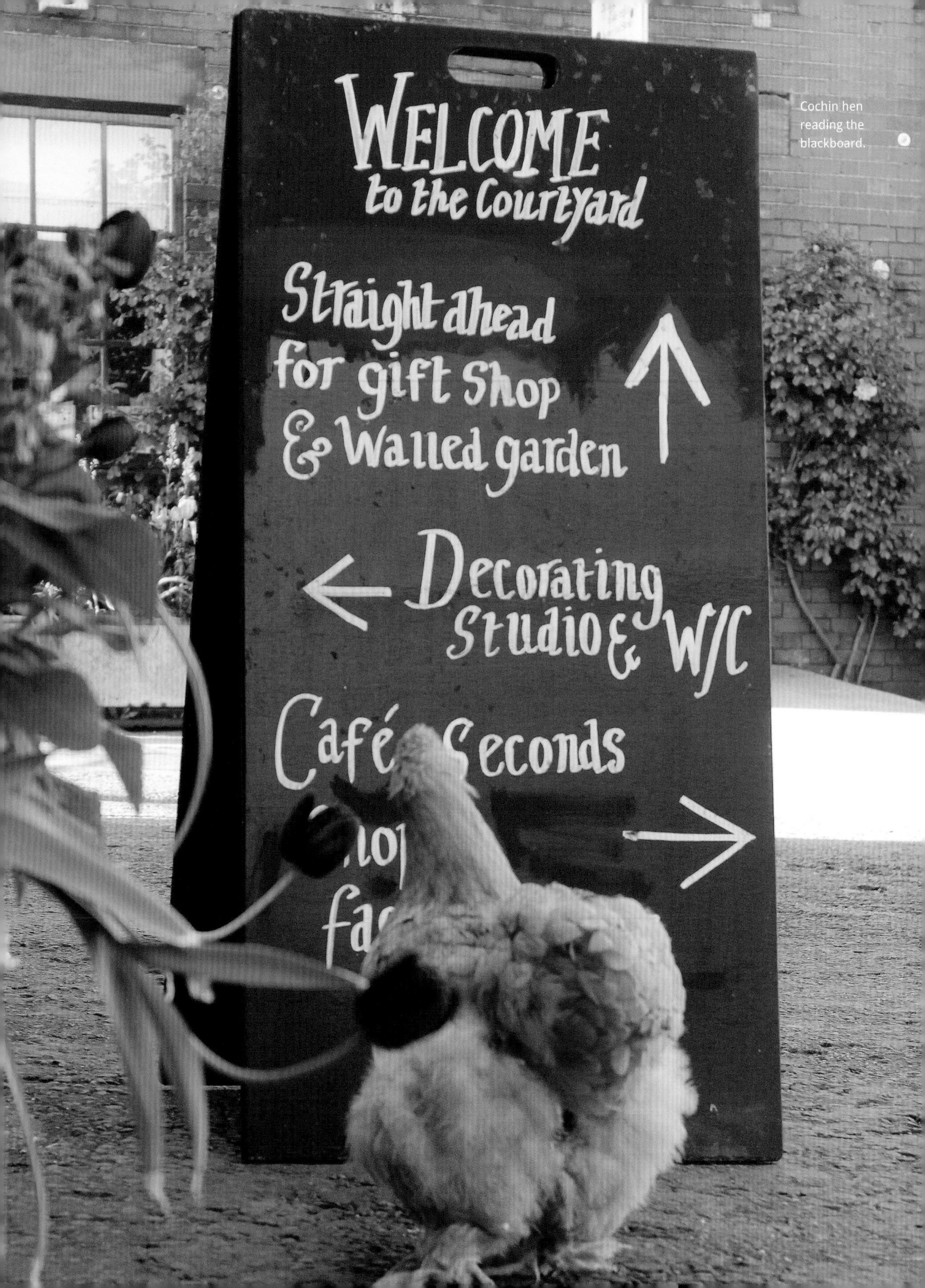

WELCOME
to the Courtyard

Straight ahead
for gift Shop
& Walled garden →

← Decorating
Studio & W/C

Café Seconds
fa→

Marzipan flowers – tulip 'Chato' with wallflower 'Sunset Apricot', tulip 'Brown Sugar' and the late narcissi 'Pheasant's Eye'.

Late spring clings on, just, but the planting of dahlias 'Bishop of Llandaff' sees the garden's attire vibrantly shift within moments to full-on summer.

Phacelia flowering with wallflowers and 'Ronaldo' tulips.

Morning glory – good, regular feeding will see them climb seemingly by the hour on warm days.

Courtyard in high summer.

ATTENTION
PARENTS

PLEASE Enjoy
the Garden with
your Children but
— PLEASE —
BEAWARE OF
THE TROUGH
POND & FREE
RANGE CHICKENS!
THANK YOU

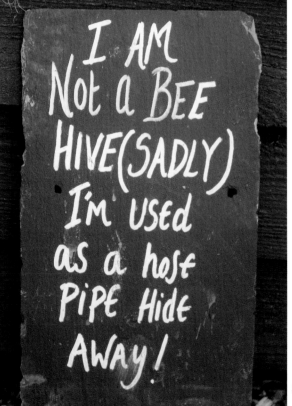

We are not Weeds,
We are Self seeded
Shirley Poppies!
Some garden flowers
refuse to become
at all domestic
& have to be
allowed to germinate
Where they like.

Cobaea scandens
also Known as the
Cup and Saucer
Plant
Will flower until
December, So its good
to Sow it in March
as it can Succeed
Sweet peas that go
over Usually by July.
FOR HALLOWEEN the
Arches are going to be draped
with PUMPKINS!

I AM
Not a BEE
HIVE (SADLY)
I'm USED
as a hose
PIPE Hide
AWAY!

A morning ritual.

PART THREE

Your Garden

Attracting Bees

It has become a fashionable and worthy thing to set aside areas of the garden as bee-friendly places – a patch where grass is left unmown and several recommended nectar-rich flowers are grown. Such places are very admirable, but what if the whole garden could be both bee attractive and beautiful, to the point that both ideas blended together seemingly without any thought? Wouldn't that be best for both the gardener and the bee?

When I lived in London, a beehive had become the must-have finishing touch for a rooftop garden. This was no bad thing, but what was needed far more than a rise in beekeepers was a rise in bee-friendly gardens bursting with welcoming, open, nectar-rich flowering plants on a large scale.

We have, as a nation, lost more than 90 per cent of our wildflower meadows, and our farmlands have become more and more intensively managed, relying in the main upon the use of harmful pesticides and herbicides. The result is a barren, flowerless landscape for our pollinating insects. The few crop flowers that are on offer to them are also largely of little help. Bees, after feasting on

Above left: Bumblebee and allium 'Violet Beauty'.

Above: Bumblebee pollinating the hardy annual *Cerinthe major* 'Purpurascens' – beautiful, but often besieged by springtime aphids, so I have a love–hate relationship with it.

Right: Dahlia 'Blue Bayou', an anemone flowering dahlia that is hugely popular with all manner of pollinating insects. Its presence will result in a summer garden that literally buzzes if planted at large.

Left: Dahlia 'Waltzing Matilda'.

Above left: *Cirsium rivulare* 'Trevor's Blue'.

Above right: Bumblebee powdered with the pollen of hollyhock 'Blackcurrant Whirl'.

large areas of the same flowering crops that have often been treated with a cocktail of chemicals, are becoming weaker and more vulnerable to diseases due to a lack of diversity in their diets. Therefore, a sanctuary for our vital bees and other pollinators can, and must, be created within our gardens.

However, this style of gardening does not mean that gardens have to become messy or meadowlike in their appearance – although a long-grass lawn is far more alive than one that is cut very short. It is the flowers that must be nectar-rich varieties in order for our backyards to become bee friendly.

I want to help all bees – those that make honey for us and the wild bumblebees (of which there are twenty-five different species) – by ensuring that the garden has a wide and abundant range of nectar-rich plants, both in the spring and, most importantly, in midsummer to late autumn when the flowers found in the countryside begin to fade and bees have to travel further and further from their hives to seek the nectar that they depend on. Bees will soon come to know of a garden that is full of nectar-rich blooms, and they will tell others in the colony on their return by doing a dance to one another to pass on the news!

Alliums, especially when planted at large, will be besieged by bees.

A balanced diet of different nectar from different flowers hugely influences the taste of honey and the health of the bee for the better too.

To ensure a welcoming feast for as many bees as possible, try to plant large swathes of similar plants, rather than a drip of this or that. The factory garden, despite being in an urban location, is, by midsummer especially, abuzz with bees of all kinds, wearing various fur jackets of the expected black, white and yellow, while others are to be seen in a tweed-brown attire with hints of apricot. Spend a few hours watching the activities of bees visiting your garden and you cannot fail to smile. For me, these summer scenes have become one of the best and most rewarding aspects of growing flowers – it's really about doing our bit to mend the damage we have done to the earth as a species with what we choose to do in our gardens. If we lose the bee then we will lose ourselves.

Almost all the plants in the factory garden, aside from the double and decorative dahlias, are bee friendly with open centres. Natural-looking flowers that don't have a profusion of double petals will allow the bees to access them more easily. Sadly, the bedding plants that are planted en masse by councils in many public spaces throughout the land at great expense are deserts to bees, being absent of nectar.

Needless to say, for a garden to be truly bee friendly, a total refrain from the use of any pesticides and herbicides must be employed. Research is only just beginning to enable us to understand the enduring repercussions of their use on soil and plants. Their effects can soak into a garden for years after they have been applied and we are only just realising the wider consequences.

Arranging Flowers

Picking flowers from your garden is one of the most beautiful things to do. But to be ruthless within a small garden for the vase on the kitchen table, leaving nothing but green outside – even if you have filled the garden with cut-and-come-again annuals – takes the heart some teaching as you'll feel like you've robbed the garden of its diamonds and jewels. This is a different and a far easier matter if you have a large garden. Areas can then be planted with flowers, for the purpose of being cut, in rows and in a part of the garden that isn't on prominent view from the back door.

Looking through the walled garden's trellis while pruning the pears in August. Echinops, the perennial globe thistle blooms, as do the perennial Japanese anemones, which some may deem far less demanding than an annual bed of cosmos. Also to be seen here are the deep plum pincushion flowers of annual scabious 'Summer Fruits' and 'Black Cat' – all are rich in nectar at a time when the bees really need it from gardens as few crops are in flower at this time.

Above: Tulips at Mill Yard.

Left: A summer flower globe. Created from a central ball of soaked oasis that is then wrapped in chicken wire, securely hung up and then stuffed with foliage before hundreds of flowers are added. Here, foraged silver birch, willow, *Cotinus coggygria* and buddleia have been mixed with supermarket gladioli. Be warned about the weight such a thing eventually ends up becoming.

I have developed a sort of middle ground with the garden's planting. Because the factory garden is relatively small and all of it is on full view, the stripping of flowers cannot usually be allowed in a harvest-like fashion; it has to be a little restrained – a flower from here and there, rather than a mowing of blooms. It's incredible how averse and shocked people can be to see me out in the garden with a pair of scissors. 'Do you have permission to pick those?' is a common question from visitors.

The nature of the Emma Bridgewater ceramic floral designs does not match the bouquets of flowers that you can normally find in the supermarket. You won't find anything that truly resembles the cottage garden wrapped in cellophane, at least not within the walls of the leading retailers. Instead, one will mostly find rigid, upright soulless blooms that have been flown in, hugely limited in choice, lacking in scent and often harbouring a cocktail of pesticides and chemicals. These don't match up to the romance that homegrown, cottage garden arrangements conjure up. The flowers need to be full of life, nostalgia and scent! However, that said, a change of tide is occurring and some supermarkets are now championing British growers

Left: Bucket of picked dahlias; care needs to be taken not to bruise their stems.

Above left: Cosmos simply picked as single stems, placed into bottles and clumped together.

Above right: Cosmos posy. A mix-up of seed packets has resulted in the white cosmos here – they should be claret!

and those who are being considerate to both the environment and their pickers abroad.

There has recently been a surge of independent florists who are stocking more romantic, seasonal blooms too. For those of us who have limited space, or are planning an event, I see no shame in buying flowers when one needs them from such outlets – few of us can afford to have the luxury of a peony walk to cut from after all! The trick is to always try to mix and match, in order to make something bought look as organic as possible.

I don't think you should fuss over arranging flowers. With time, arranging will become a simple, quick, rhythmic ritual that you get better at and, with a selection of personal vases you know, you'll learn the heights and forms of flowers that each vessel can support. For me, plonking flowers in several vases is arranging. The result needs to be beautiful and striking, but it can be simple too. Often less is more. Let the flowers speak for themselves, keep their stems decently tall, let them have a life. Give them a vase that suits – it doesn't have to be a huge one, nothing is sadder-looking than a vase which seems to be half-full of blooms. Instead, arrange single stems with a consort

of foliage sprigs into mugs and recycle beautifully shaped glass bottles and other vintage finds.

If you do want to do a knockout, full-on large vase arrangement, then keep in mind the shape of a peacock's fanned-out tail feathers being displayed on a slightly windy day. Always start with the foliage first and then the flowers, placing them like the feathered eyes of the peacock's train in a uniform fashion – some high, some central, some low. Stand back and look for gaps that need to be filled with a flowering pop of colour, until you are pleased with the look. The hard part, having grown the flowers yourself, has been done – the picking and arranging part is like setting off a firework and bringing it inside!

Spring is the hardest time to produce cut flowers because tulips and other bulbs are not cut-and-come-again. Once the flower is picked, that's a segment of the garden robbed of its beauty, which cannot be recreated until next spring. Often the café and shops are so hot, with it still being winter-coat weather for the customers, that the poor cut dears flop over in despair within a weekend and I'll return on Monday morning feeling guilty and angry, knowing that, had I not cut them, they would still be looking resplendent out in the garden, while inside they have moulted their petals prematurely.

Foraging helps endlessly in filling a vase up. People get nervous over whether it's legal. Of course you can't walk into the local park and start hacking away at lilac and cherry blossom and expect that to go unnoticed, nor would it be right to do so, but if you open your eyes to areas of derelict land, where all sorts of self-seeded and neglected flora can be found, a lot can be cut without offending anyone.

By early summer, things get far less guilt-ridden when it comes to picking flowers properly from the garden, as the sweet peas, half-hardy annuals and dahlias come into play. These are cut-and-come-again and they grow fast. In fact, cutting them when they are in flower ensures that they'll continue to produce more flowers. If you don't 'live-head' these plants by cutting their flowers for the vase then you'll have to deadhead them as their flowers fade – so it's a no-brainer to me. I'd rather be cutting something beautiful to take into the shop than have a shop bare of flowers and a wheelbarrow full of faded blooms in high summer.

The important thing is to know where to cut a flower from – you can't just hack the main stem off and expect flowers to be there the next week, as you'll have cut off the plant's main structure and it will try to regrow this before

Opposite top: Dahlia 'Mel's Marmalade' with blue hydrangea.

Far left: Cosmos 'Rubenza'.

Left: Seed-grown dahlias 'Bishops Children'.

flowering again. What you want to do is cut down to a plant's armpits. These are the joints that go down to the main stem or where a pair of leaves can be seen. From these joints and leaf pairs, the plant will quickly grow axillary buds which will become the next harvest of flowers in the coming weeks.

Also, you need to ensure that you're going to get the maximum vase life out of any flowers that you're going to cut from the garden and arrange in a way that makes it worthwhile. Following these steps will see many flowers last for at least four days to a week once they have been cut:

- Pick in the early morning or evening, never in the heat of midday.
- Pick flowers into a bucket of water. If you have to carry them without water, hold the flowers upside down with their heads downwards. This way, the moisture in their stems will go towards the flower's head.
- If you can, leave the picked flowers overnight in a deep bucket of water somewhere cool – a garage or pantry – so that they can have a long drink before being arranged the next day.
- Strip all foliage that is going to be below the water level of the vase from the flower's stem – foliage under water will quickly cause the water to sour.
- To help keep the water clean and limit bacterial growth, add a glug of vodka to a big vase or a shot-glass worth to a small one. There are lots of opinions about what is the best addition to water to keep flowers alive the longest, but vodka I have found to be the best, as alcohol is anti-bacterial. Lemonade is said to be of help, but its sugar is an aid to bacteria. A copper penny is now useless as modern ones lack enough bronze in their make-up to be of any proper aid.
- Sear the last few inches of the ends of hardwood flower stems – roses, lilac and also sappy ones like bluebells and euphorbia – in just-off-the-boil water for 30 seconds. The hot, boiling water exfoliates the stems' pores so they can absorb more water. After 30 seconds, plunge them into cold water straight away.
- Don't expect any flowers to last in warm rooms. If you can, put vases of flowers outside overnight and leave them outside if you're going to be away from home for the day. I think it's good to have a large arrangement outside on a table that you can see from the kitchen window and just have bud vases inside so that the magnificence of a large arrangement can last as long as possible.

Top: Autumn arrangement of hedgerow foliage and blackberries, the annual rudbeckia 'Cherry Brandy' and dahlias 'Happy Halloween', 'Bishop of Llandaff' and 'Chat Noir' at Perch Hill.

Far left: Arrangement of the decorative dahlia 'Indian Summer' with the perennial rudbeckia 'Goldstrum'. Their primary colours match the dominance of the staple Emma Bridgewater polka-dot pattern.

Left: Sweet peas in a polka-dot jug.

A dried winter arrangement using dried allium heads, hydrangea as a dense base and dried sprigs of skeletal cow parsley.

Dahlias in glass goblets with acid-green *Euphorbia oblongata* sprigs.

Alliums arranged with nepeta 'Six Hills Giant' in recycled bottles, creating a quick, simple but effective window ledge display.

103

Party flowers in bud vases fill the barn at Perch Hill. Cosmos, calendula, opium poppies, Iceland poppies and snapdragons all massed in single bud vases for maximum impact.

Tulips massed together in single vases within a basket at Perch Hill.

Buddleia and sunflower 'Earthwalker'.

Searing stems.

Tulips at Mill Yard filling
a hanging chandelier
using a small soaked
ball of oasis sitting in its
heart.

Goblet of annuals.

Allium Schubertii sprayed golden for Christmas.

Plucked flamingos – dahlias 'Labyrinth' and 'Selina' being given a drink overnight before being arranged.

Bottles of single stems on a windowsill of the café – panicum 'Frosted Explosion', dahlias and cosmos. Heated rooms are one of the main reasons flowers fade within days.

Keeping Poultry

The most beautiful dress I have seen Emma wear is one that has a pattern, top to bottom, of black and white Sebright Bantam lacing.

My gardening habits have been shaped around chickens as I like to have the hens out with me for at least an hour a day. For this reason, I keep mostly Bantams. Their small feet do less harm when they are amongst the plants than the scratching, soil-churning actions of the bigger egg-laying breeds, but some of the largest fluffy Asiatic varieties are good for the garden too.

The bore of raising chicks via incubator and heat lamp is highlighted when their artificial upbringing is compared to the ease at which a broody hen can do the whole task of sitting and rearing her clutch of chicks with the minimum of worry. Such a natural picture of a mother hen and her chicks is the highlight of a factory visit for many in the summer. Occasionally, such feathered families in the garden may also contain fostered ducklings, as if they were out of a Beatrix Potter watercolour farmyard scene.

There isn't space to go into all details of poultry rearing here, so I've only included the basics to understand and consider, plus a handful of my favourite breeds of hens and a mention of keeping ducks.

While Deborah Devonshire was certainly my hen-keeping idol, it was Victoria Roberts' video called *Poultry at Home* that was my weekend education on poultry husbandry. Victoria's opening line, 'Would you like fresh eggs every day, something for the table on Sunday or a hobby to interest the children?', boomed through Mill Yard several times each Saturday and Sunday for many years. My mum, as a result, knows Victoria's very informative script as well as I do.

Hens

Time

Just like any form of livestock or pet, hens need daily feeding and checking. If their hen house is not within the security of a fox-proof run, they'll need to be let out in the morning and put away each evening before dark.

Week-old Buff Cochin chicks; their characteristic fluffy trousers are already noticeable.

Feeding Hens

Chickens are omnivores, they eat both meat and plants. Their daily feeding is straightforward, consisting mainly of layers' pellets and grain. Solid pellets are better than traditional mash as this sticks to the hens' beaks, resulting in their water getting dirty quickly when they then go to take a drink. Crazily, you cannot legally feed kitchen scraps to hens anymore, but cabbage leaves and garden weeds (such as dandelions) hung up in a wire wild-bird fat ball feeder will provide much excitement as well as some fresh goodness. For digestion and eggshell production, hens need to be given specialist poultry grit which contains oyster shell.

Like dogs and cats, hens benefit from being wormed so that they are not burdened with internal parasites which can cause weight loss and reduced egg laying. These worms are carried in slugs and snails, so do not deliberately feed them to your chickens. The poultry medication 'Flubenvet', fed twice a year through medicated layers' pellets, will help ensure healthy birds.

Always feed your hens in hanging feeders so that they can't spill feed as they peck. Ensure that there is never any feed left in the feeders each evening

Above: The most thrilling of eggs to collect, Maran eggs.

Right: Hanging up greens, such as the heads of sunflowers and garden weeds, will provide much excitement for hens that are kept confined.

as this will attract rats. Galvanised metal feeders look far nicer on the eye than the cheaper plastic sort. And are far more robust! You can also buy feeders that store several days' worth of feeding that won't encourage vermin. To access the feed, the hens have to stand on a platform that acts as a pedal. With their weight on it, the otherwise closed feeding gulley opens, allowing them to gain access to the feed. Such feeders are good if you are working on early and late shifts and need to let the hens feed themselves liberally.

Fine Feathers

To keep themselves clean and neat, chickens dustbathe in dry soil. They will fluff up their feathers so that the earth gets onto their skin, helping to deter mites. Hens need to be given dry sand in a deep plastic tray so that they can carry out this important behaviour. For hens allowed into the garden, keep hedge bottoms and other dry soil areas free from planting so that the birds can easily make their own dust baths, and so they don't begin to make their own amongst the plants.

Above: Broody Bantams, Lavender Pekin, Buff Orpington and a Wyandotte cross dustbathing before they begin their twenty-one days of sitting, various eggs having arrived on loan from my friend Vicki. Dustbathing is a very important thing for hens to do if they are to remain healthy and contented.

Above left: A Chamois Poland cockerel with a gold-laced Wyandotte and Araucana hen of uncertain ancestry.

Above right: Pekin Bantams, white and buff, peeking out from their hen house at Chatsworth Farmyard.

Once a year, hens will moult, losing their feathers and growing a new set. Mix cod liver oil and seaweed powder into their layers' pellets to help them grow shiny new plumage quickly.

Point of Lay

This is the age that young hens are normally sold at, being around 18 weeks old. During this age they are known as pullets. Most hens will begin to lay their first eggs from around 20 weeks old, depending on the time of year and their breed. They will also be sold as sexed hens at this age as they can be told apart from young cockerels with certainty by experienced breeders. Young hens have smaller combs, are less red in their faces and have smaller feet than young cockerels.

A hen's natural lifespan is around five to seven years. Most hens lay at their best during the spring and summer, because it is the length of daylight that stimulates egg laying.

Christopher, the Buff Cochin cockerel, free-ranging. Anchusa 'Dropmore', a semi-perennial relation to the annual borage but of a more intense peacock blue, is in full flower here with sage and foxgloves.

At times poultry have to be kept penned for the sake of the garden. A solid coop has a concrete floor which is helpful in that it deters rats. It is bedded down with a thick layer of good quality, absorbent wood shavings and is cleaned out weekly.

We are not allowed to Free range at the Moment We have been Pecking the Plants far to Much!

Pecking Order

Hens live in a strict hierarchy that can be hard for us to stomach. Bullying is part of it, but once order is reached this eases as each bird, from top to bottom, knows her place within the flock. Displacing this way of chicken life by introducing new hens to the flock can cause great discontentment within the ranks. For newcomers to stand a chance, they should be of the same age as the resident hens and be introduced in (at least) pairs, not singletons, and they should be put together with your original birds at dusk, so that they all awake together, causing less of a shock.

Note: young birds cannot be put straight in with older hens as they will be terrorised and may even be killed.

Home to Roost

A hen house needs to be light and airy, but also cosy. Small arks are fine for a pair of birds but far better is a converted shed that you can stand up in and then you won't have to be constantly bending down to access. The hens will want a solid, square-sided perch to roost on and a dark nesting box, full of straw. Their litter is best being a dusting of dust-extracted wood shavings, as this is absorbent. (Hen manure makes a very good mulch for the vegetable garden, but needs to be turned often and takes a year to properly rot down.)

Raise the hen house a good foot off the floor so that rats can't burrow underneath.

New hens need to be shut in their hen house when they arrive to their new home so that they know where to go the following evening, once they have been let out for the first time.

Cockerels

You don't need a cockerel for the hens to lay eggs. Close neighbours, sadly, may not appreciate its crowing either! A cockerel's presence does help to ease tensions a little between the hens, with a mature male asserting himself as head of the flock. Without one treading them, the hens will often crouch down with their wings spread as you approach, just as they would do to a cockerel advancing towards them.

Opposite top: Wyandottes. Hens need to be transported calmly, in sturdy boxes.

Right: Buff Cochin hen. Feeders that hang at pecking height will help hugely in limiting the amount of feed spilt on to the floor.

Far right: Sarah's old speckled hen at Perch Hill.

It is important to check your house deeds before buying any chickens, as some areas don't allow the keeping of any livestock in an urban setting.

Chicken Run

A permanent run attached to the hen house is important to keep the birds secure and to spare your garden from their constant activities. Hen droppings, when fresh, are acidic, so a small lawn will suffer with a traditional, movable hen run placed on it – even if this is moved around daily. Such systems are suited to large orchards where space gives areas of grass time to recover.

Hens dislike the wind and rain. Their ancestors are small and pheasant-like, and are known as jungle fowl, who are native to the subtropical woodlands of Asia. From this natural setting, our modern breeds have all carried in their genes a dislike of being in the open and exposed to the elements. Nothing is worse for chickens than damp and muddy conditions that they cannot get out of. Hens love to sunbathe, so site the run in a place that catches full sun for part of the day.

To keep out the wet, a run can have a solid roof of Perspex plastic sheeting that will still allow the sunlight in but will stop wild birds, who could bring disease, from visiting. Choose strong, galvanised chicken wire, not the cheaper and thin sort, so foxes cannot bite through it. A hen run needs to be totally fox-proof and the hens are best kept locked in it if you're away from home all day.

Wood chippings are a good floor covering for the run as they will prevent mud and stale ground if replaced several times a year – the spent chippings will make a good mulch. Logs and thick branches will be enjoyed as outside perching.

Powder

Dust the entire inside of the hen house monthly, especially the perches and nesting boxes, with a natural powder called Diatomaceous Earth. This grey powder prevents the infestation of a nocturnal parasite that sucks the hens' blood – the dreaded red mite. These mites live in the dark areas of the henhouse during the day and come out to feed in the dark as they sense the warmth of the roosting hens. The bright light of a mobile phone is very helpful for inspecting the dark corners of a hen house!

A regal Buff Pekin hen with deep-tangerine plumage accompanied by a Lavender Pekin cockerel at Chatsworth Farmyard. These birds are ideal for both small and large gardens, and they have huge personalities.

Manicures

Give your hens monthly leg massages of Vaseline smeared well into their scales to keep their legs sleek! Breeds with feathered legs will need to be given warm foot baths in the winter so that they don't get clagged with mud. Their fluffy bottom feathers may also need to be lightly trimmed too.

Gardening with Hens

Hens will peck and scratch, it's what they do every minute of the day until they go to roost, so they are not a match made in heaven for the English garden to host. Some plants will fare far better than others and these include alliums, woody herbs like sage, rosemary and lavender, artichokes, bearded iris, perennial grasses, roses, crocosmia and most flowering shrubs. Protecting areas of the garden so that the hens cannot gain access can be achieved decoratively with woven birch and hessian pea netting.

Breeds

There are so many different breeds of chickens that it can be a perplexing task to make an informed, firm choice as to which ones you should keep to suit you and your garden. The best thing to do is visit an open farm that keeps a good range of chicken breeds, so that you can see what several breeds look and act like in their natural setting. Then, having seen them in the flesh and picked out some that you like, research these breeds as much as you can before finding any for sale and deciding to buy.

Don't buy hens from auctions, where birds may be bought cheaply but are often in poor condition. Instead, track down dedicated breeders or buy young stock from rare breed farm parks. Poultry shows are good to attend too, just to see the egg-entry classes alone, but the true character of the breeds cannot always be determined when seeing them as trained birds, all posed in cages, while they wait to be judged. Such places, however, are where breeders and breed clubs will give good information to prospective keepers that only those with years of knowing individual breeds can offer.

I am an advocate of keeping the rare and pure breeds, but the crossbred, commercially kept, hard-laying hybrid hens offer an easy introduction for many into what becomes a lifetime of hen keeping. Certain hens, including

Above left: A
Welsummer hen.

Above right: A duckling
fostered to a lavender
Pekin Bantam hen and
her chicks. Ducks need a
pond so, alas, their time
in a garden absent of a
proper one is limited.

the hybrids especially, are very good layers but they are then terrors if let into
the garden, while those that look pretty often just lay small eggs in sparing
numbers. So you have to weigh up the pros and cons of whether you want
something behind or in front of the chicken wire.

Cochins

Cochins – my favourites – in their buff champagne feather colour, are often
mistaken for the more commonly kept Buff Orpingtons. The main differences
between these two giants amongst chicken breeds is that the Cochins have
feathered, pantaloon trouser legs while Orpingtons carry themselves in a
similar low fashion, but have bare legs and are a little less fluffy in appearance.
Cochins are the ultimate teddy-bear-like chickens!

The Buff Cochins were made famous for several decades by Deborah
Devonshire keeping them at Chatsworth, with flocks to be seen free-ranging
in the gardens during her time as Duchess of Devonshire. Her Grace once

Opposite top: Pair of black Pekin Bantams, Chatsworth farmyard.

Far left: Warren hybrid hens in the white interior of the poultry house at Chatsworth farmyard.

Left: Deborah Devonshire's former hen house, the Game Larder, at Chatsworth House today. Now magnificently restored, its beautiful mosaic floor can be seen again, having once been protected by wood shavings and hen droppings. The building became a hen house after it was dismissed as being too small for anything of use, in terms of being a shop or a café, and plans show that it once had a domed roof. A great many pure breed chickens are to be found still at large in the nearby Chatsworth farmyard. The farmyard was opened in 1973 by the duchess after she noticed that visiting school children and teachers alike had little idea about the realities of farming or the use of farm animals. It continues to fulfill this important and vital purpose.

used them as opening props as a replacement to flowers during a dinner party, hosting the visiting fashion designer Óscar de la Renta.

Perhaps surprisingly to hen newcomers, the gentle-looking hens will not lay many eggs. A Cochin hen will lay just a few dozen small, tinted eggs each year. The breed was originally bred in China, reared for the purpose of fluffy feathers to stuff cushions with, rather than egg production. Cochins are hugely docile in their character. They rarely get into a flapping state and will bring a large garden to life with steady movement. The hens will become broody, but they are so clumsy that during a hen's sitting several eggs may be squashed, especially if they are of a small size. But they do make very good foster mothers to larger goose eggs. Their heavy nature means that they won't enjoy having to climb into a hen house that requires any form of ladder!

As young chicks, the Cochins take a long time to feather up, taking a full year of growing to reach a mature look – compared to the speed of other breeds, this is very slow. A good diet and more time under a heat lamp (so they don't get chilled) will ensure that they rear well into adulthood.

Cochins don't just come in a buff colour; they can be also found in white, black, partridge, cuckoo, blue and mottled.

Marans and Welsummers

Deep-brown eggs always seem to be the most delectable when they are seen amongst other shades of eggs gathered in the kitchen, and even more so when discovering them laid, awaiting collection in the nesting box. The French Cuckoo Maran – the original old speckled hen – and the pretty Dutch-bred Welsummer make up the two most famed pure-breed layers of deep-chocolate-brown (Maran) and rich plant-pot terracotta (Welsummer) eggs. The full-bodied Maran hen is more placid in her nature than the sometimes aloof Welsummer.

To seek out young hens (pullets), who will lay good numbers of their much-admired eggs, a breeder who breeds specifically for egg production rather than for showing must be sought. The breeders of these hens will be very eager to show off the deep-shelled pedigrees of their adult breeding birds and you should always ask to check on this because it is only female chicks from hens mated with cockerels of dark egg strains that will go onto lay deep-brown eggs themselves.

These hens should be given roomy runs and not fed too much corn as they are liable to become overweight, which will cause lazy laying.

The Welsummer cockerel is like a moving bed of 'Persian Carpet' wallflowers with fierce talons!

The hybrid layer known as the Speckledy has been bred from the Maran.

Pekin Bantams

Rounded, small and cuddly, Pekin Bantams are the best hens for the garden. They paddle through the flower beds causing little mess, due to their foot feathers and small size, and become very tame with large personalities. They have become very popular as pet hens recently and this has resulted in their breed standards varying hugely from what they were originally. These little birds should be low to the floor and not upright in their stance, the ideal Pekin hen is said to resemble a cup and saucer!

The hens lay small white eggs and distracting them from broodiness can be a problem in the summer. The cockerels are delightfully proud and gentle to their hens. Originally bred in China, in America they are known as Cochin Bantams, due to their similarities to the larger Cochin. Pekin Bantams have been bred into a huge array of colours, including buff, white, black, cuckoo, lavender, partridge and Columbian.

Warren hybrids

Bred from the pure American Rhode Island Red, these hard-working girls are now the most popular industrial layers of supermarket brown eggs. They will lay an egg almost every day for their first two seasons, literally tiring themselves out, hence they have a commercial farm life that is often less than twelve months. They were not really bred for the outside cold, being loosely feathered and never really looking properly neat, but they become very tame and are easy-going.

They are available cheaply as young hens and will duly start laying for you within weeks of settling in, or you can rehome them as retired battery farm girls. These ladies will be in a shocking state after their intensive start, often being badly pecked, but the joy of watching them regrow their feathers and then enjoying a proper, free-range life is hugely rewarding. They go under a

Pekin Bantams.

huge array of names – I was introduced to them as Warrens, but they are also known as Hissex Browns and Hylines. The pure-breed Rhode Island Red that these hens have been bred from are larger and a rich mahogany brown.

Other breeds for the garden and for eggs
Garden – Silkie, Bantam Wyandotte, Poland, Belgian Bantam, Brahma.
Eggs – Sussex, Leghorn, Cream Legbar, Hamburg, Black Rock (hybrid).

Ducks

Ducks seem to appeal far more to visitors than the chickens. Perhaps it is their kinder faces, with rounded bodies and beaks, and comical waddling. Ducks are, visually at least, nicer to one another than chickens, with very little pecking. They seem to go about their day without fuss and in contentment.

Ducks are true waterfowl and need water, which means that they create mud. Their dabbling activities begin to brown the grass and expose the mud (which will keep them amused for hours). And they'll plonk themselves amongst plants to sleep, flattening down delicate clumps.

Large classical puddle ducks such as the Aylesbury are too big for a garden, but their smaller, daintier cousins can suit a garden space far better. Breeds such as Black East Indians, Miniature Crested Appleyards and the constantly quacking rubber-duck-like Call Ducks can all be considered as possibilities. They won't lay many eggs, however – the females will only lay several clutches in late spring.

No ducks, sadly, will suit a formal waterlily pond of a modest garden size – they will soon ruin it. Ducks need their own swimming bath. This does not need to be a huge expanse of water, but it must allow them to fully submerge themselves for a proper paddle so that they can stay clean and not develop eye and foot problems. The easiest form of duck pond to create is a large tin bath that can be emptied and refilled with clean water each day. The factory garden has a drain and, with its base being gravel on top of concrete, mud doesn't accumulate, so place a duck bath at home on a similar type of surface.

Opposite top: Young ducks with their pin feathers pushing through their duckling down.

Far left: Hatching duck egg.

Left: Regular access to clean water for bathing and submerging their heads is vital for ducks. A tin bath makes an attractive duck pond that is easy to empty and refill.

A broad, wooden, gently sloping ladder will allow the birds access to bathing at their leisure.

For those who have to keep their ducks penned, keeping mud at bay is more difficult, unless the run's base can be of solid concrete and near a drain so that their duck bath can be emptied. The concrete floor will need to be covered over with a soft bed of straw, which will then have to be changed every few days.

I hatch ducks out each spring in an incubator. Their blue or white eggs take twenty-eight days to hatch. The eggs are misted daily with water to help soften the egg's inner membrane. Ducklings quickly imprint on the first thing that they see moving, so those that are raised artificially become incredibly tame towards people. Broody chickens will foster day-old ducklings as long as they are put underneath them when their own eggs are hatching. Mother hens develop a photographic memory of what their brood consists of within the first twenty-four hours of leaving the nest so, before this, fostered ducklings can be smuggled in underneath their feathers!

Ducklings taking their first swim amongst floating flowers in a glass trifle bowl.

Ducklings are given short and shallow swimming lessons from their first day, but these have to be supervised as the youngsters don't become waterproof until a few months old. Until then, they are liable to become fatally chilled.

Young Bantam ducklings are good when they are a week old to be used as slug patrol within a flower bed. Slugs and snails are hosts to internal parasites that infest chickens, but ducks don't seem to become affected by having them in their diets.

Ducklings grow fast, seemingly changing into ducks by the day. They keep their baby-soft down until their adult feathers appear from underneath, with their bellies becoming properly plumed up first.

Ducks are happy to be fed a diet based on wheat and their meals can be fed to them in a shallow tray full of water so they can spend time filtering it up with their beaks. A treat for ducks is cut-up lettuce, garden weeds and, most of all, aquatic duckweed put into water creating a watery salad.

Once ducks have grown their flight feathers, their light bodies may see them begin to fly. To prevent an escape, some of the duck's primary wing feathers will need to be clipped by cutting several of these large feathers back halfway in their length on one wing, just lightly. As long as the feathers are not cut back more than halfway, then the process doesn't hurt the bird. It's similar to us having our finger nails cut, and the same method is used on unruly hens that learn to fly over hedges and chicken wire – the wing clipping renderers them unbalanced in the air and they are therefore unable to take off properly.

Ducks don't need perches as they'll sleep on the floor, but they do need a secure house to reside in at night with a dry bed of straw. Hens will dislike their wet habits so don't house them together!

PART FOUR

Seasonal Plants and Jobs

Laying out bulbs to be planted.

Spring

The emergence of crocus signals winter's grip slowly loosening on the factory garden; however, until the narcissi have faded I always keep a jumper close to hand. It is the flowering of the late tulips that herald spring's official coronation; the hens begin to lay more as dawn slowly peeks in earlier and earlier, and the first seeds of spring that I sow in the greenhouse are the cobeae in March. The freshness and zest of May is my favourite time of year, when everything is new and bright, and the hours spent bulb planting in the dark are rewarded time and time again by new shoots. The month of May also sees me setting eggs for incubation, with the promise of new life of a different kind.

The two courtyard beds along the café and seconds shop walls.

March Checklist

Sow tender-climbing annuals such as cup and saucer plant (*Cobaea scandens*), morning glory (*Ipomoea*) and black-eyed Susan (*Thunbergia*). Don't be tempted to sow other things yet in the north – wait until April.

Plant bare-root roses now, if you've not done so earlier in the year, and mulch around those already in the ground. Do both these tasks in mild weather.

Pinch out the growth tips of sweet peas once the young plants develop five pairs of leaves to encourage bushing.

Directly sow the crimson flowering broad bean.

If you've not already done so, prune buddleias back hard to encourage a later flowering towards the end of July when butterflies will be in need of their nectar more than earlier in the season.

Continue to keep hens off the flower beds as the crowns of perennials begin to emerge – their sprouts being too tempting for beaks to ignore! Deliberately catch and cuddle cockerels often – as their hormones rise, this show of dominance between bird and keeper will reduce the chances of a boot-chasing cockerel! You can protect flower beds neatly by using 2ft-high pea and bean jute netting.

Now the weather is warming, dust the hen house weekly with generous amounts of Diatomaceous Earth to combat the parasitic red mite. For pullets coming into lay, show them the correct places to lay by supplying fake pottery eggs in the nest box.

December-sown sweet peas will be stronger plants than those sown in the spring.

March

Plant Profile: Climbers

HALF-HARDY ANNUALS – SOW IN MARCH FOR FLOWERS FROM JULY TO OCTOBER

Several of these more exotic plants need to be sown early in the year (March) at a high propagation temperature to ensure that they germinate successfully. Once they have germinated, they are usually fast growing and will soon want a stick in their pots to begin climbing upwards. They will flower as the sweet peas fade from July, if not before.

Black-Eyed Susan (Thunbergia alata)

My favourite is the 'Sunset Shades' mix that has every shade of sunny yellow, apricot and orange, with striking black middles and healthy green foliage. Sow them in March, as they take the best part of a month to germinate (propagator heat will help). The seedlings can then be slow to really get themselves going, sulking for a week or so after being pricked out of the seed tray, but they will perk up. Bees adore them and they will look good into October or November.

Cup and Saucer Plant (Cobaea scandens)

A real jungle-looking flower to me it is the untamed version of a morning glory. It is a very late-flowering climber, beginning to flower from the end of July and then going on into December. It will cover walls and arches

quickly. Its flowering stems are long enough for it to be used as a cut flower too. In sheltered places such as cities, and if the plant is well established, it may even overwinter outside if the climate is mild. It can also be grown as a climbing conservatory plant.

As seedlings, ensure that they never become thirsty while in their pots. Sow in early March – a heated propagator will be of help to speed germination.

Runner Bean

A helpful, fast-growing banker. If grown for a crop of beans, they need to be sown in April, but for just decorative use they can be sown in June. The large seeds can be directly sown and will grow quickly.

While I cannot abide the taste of the bean, the flowers of some varieties can be very decorative and the leaves will a give lush coverage to anything that their stems can wrap themselves around.

Clockwise from top left:
The broad bean flowers are very bee attractive and also edible.

Thunbergia alata 'African Sunset' flowers into late October with gusto.

Morning glory – by midday its blooms will have become limp, with the next day's flowers fattening up behind them.

Cobaea scandens flowering in November.

Foliage Profile: Globe Artichoke and Cardoon

These provide soft, yet architectural foliage from March, then if allowed to flower the tall flowering stalks give huge impact from June and on into the winter if not cut down. They can be grown from seed in March/April, but more rapid establishment will be seen from bought-in plants.

Their foliage is invaluable, emerging early in March. I pick it all the year round for arranging. The silver-blue colour and arching habit of their leaves is incredibly useful for arrangements, both of small and large scale.

The cardoon is hardier and quicker in its growth than the artichoke for northern gardens.

When their globular flowers do open, seemingly like a goblet relic from ancient Rome, they will be visited by bees and butterflies in abundance as they drink the plentiful nectar dry from the violet hearts. You can also cut the golden-brown seed heads down and take them into the house to dry. Several stems placed into a heavy-based vase can be festooned with copper-wired fairy lights for Christmas.

Plant Profile: Plume Thistle (Cirsium rivulare) 'Atropurpureum'

A stalwart of the Chelsea Flower Show, with its thistle-like leaves and stems giving way to the most beautiful claret flower head, these will be besieged by bumblebees. The plume thistle is the tamed and wanted version of *Bill and Ben*, the Flower Pot Men's mischievous thistle character.

Buy in an adult plant, then divide this perennial in early spring once the clump has become mature after several seasons. They flower normally by May and on into June. If they are cut down in August, they may flower again in mid-autumn. The purchase of one plant (they don't seem to grow from seed) will see a good-sized clump grow within a few seasons that can then be divided to create more. They like dappled shade and soil that doesn't dry out, hence one of their common names being 'brook thistle'.

Opposite Top: Artichoke flower heads look like huge reptilian eggs cut with fronds of fennel. The flower heads often retain their blue central colour and will look beautiful inside for years; they look brilliant sprayed with gold paint for Christmas too.

Right: Bumblebee with heavy pollen sacs feasting on *Cirsium rivulare* flowering in the courtyard.

Far right: *Cirsium rivulare* 'Atropurpureum'.

Cosmos seedlings pricked out. Half-hardy annuals grow very quickly, filling pots within weeks of being pricked out from a seed tray. As such, it is easier to sow them in late rather than early spring, as none can be planted into the garden until all risk of late frosts have passed.

April Checklist

Begin to sow cosmos and sunflowers (under cover) now as the month progresses, with the aim of having most seedlings pricked out and growing well in 9cm pots for the beginning of May for hardening off. Pinch the tips off the majority of seedlings once they are 5in tall or have five pairs of leaves.

Towards the end of the month pot up dahlia tubers – one tuber to a 3-litre pot. Water their compost sparingly to begin with.

Plant bulbs of gladioli, continuing to do so on a monthly basis until June for a good succession of their flowers.

Lily bulbs can be planted now too, again under cover and in pots to be planted out into the garden once summer arrives properly.

Water pots of tulips; their flowers will crisp up and fade prematurely should their pots become too dry.

Apply biological slug controls to the garden to protect plants such as dahlias from slugs and snails in the coming weeks – a combined organic approach using nematodes and then placing wool pellets and sharp grit around freshly planted out plants should work well.

Move self-sown thugs such as teasel while they are still small, should they be in inconvenient spots.

Plant out sweet pea seedlings by the middle of the month.

Comb through perennial grasses to get rid of built-up dead material within their centres and, if required, cut them back.

Treat yourself by picking some of the tulips from the garden. Do this early in the day and give them a long drink in a tall upright bucket overnight to maximise their vase life before arranging. Pick them with wallflowers, euphorbia and artichokes for a full-looking arrangement that doesn't require masses of tulips for a lavish look.

Direct sow blue or purple tansy (*Phacelia tanacetifolia*) in areas where tulips are cleared from the border after they've finished flowering, or sow it as you plant out your half-hardy annuals later in May.

April

Plant Profile: Cosmos

HALF-HARDY ANNUAL – SOW IN APRIL FOR FLOWERS FROM JUNE TO NOVEMBER

A packet of cosmos seed would probably be what I would choose over any other packet of seeds – if I was forced to pick just one to grow for summer flowers – both for its virtues as a garden plant and as a cut flower. This half-hardy annual, being originally native to Mexico, is incredibly easy to grow from seed. Sow in April for June flowers. Once they are in flower (by the middle of June), the blooms are loosely held above green feather-duster-like foliage. The flowers are gently swaying, delicate yet attention grabbing, with their petals enclosing a bright-yellow centre that is rich in nectar for all manner of pollinators. Cosmos will flower their socks off until the first frost of winter. Their flowers can be cut for the house every week and this will spur the plants on to become bushier and ever more flower-productive.

Left: Dahlia 'Blue Bayou' with the semi-double cosmos 'Click Cranberries'. The lantern-like seed pod and flower buds of *Nicandra physalodes* and the deep flowers of the salvia 'Amistad' gives depth to the combination, despite them all being of a similar colour tone.

Bumblebee on a freshly opened cosmos 'Antiquity'.

Plant Profile: Gladiolus

You have to be cautious of the mainstream gladioli and only buy varieties that your eyes have actually seen in flower for themselves. If you plant the right ones, however, then you won't regret it. Your garden will be amassed with the most lavish, velvet spires of intense colour rocketing upwards, taking the summer show into the most exotic, vertical dimension.

Plant corms from April to June for successional flowers from July to October. Aside from staking them individually as the heavy flower spikes begin to bloom, gladioli need little attention once they are growing well and the hens won't peck at them! Summer-flowering gladioli are considered to be tender, but I've left them in the ground for the past few years and they have reappeared happily each spring

The hardy, more delicate 'Byzantine' (*Gladiolus communis subsp. Byzantinus*) is a species gladiolus. Unlike its more brassy-bred cousins, it is planted in the autumn with its bulbs being noticeably smaller and hardy. Its delicate, orchid-like form and much-needed garden appearance at this time of year, during the May to June gap, means that I plant more of these each autumn.

It looks at its relaxed best within a meadow. Here, when left undisturbed and allowed to die back after its flowering with grace amongst long unmown grass, it will normally prove to be perennial.

Clockwise from top left:
Gladiolus 'Purple Flora'.

Gladiolus 'Espresso'.

Gladiolus 'Magma' takes the garden into September with punch, along with nicandra, salvia 'Amistad', cosmos 'Rubenza', red millet, flowering bronze fennel and the fronds and cobs of the sweetcorn 'Popcorn Fiesta'.

Gladiolus 'Plum Tart'.

Plant Profile: Dahlia

Once banished as a flower for agricultural show cut-flower classes, and seen back then as an animal of hospital-wall pastel colours and grotesque size, today this Mexican native is one of the most productive and classiest of flowers to grow.

The dahlia is a bloom that has the capability to transform both the smallest of balconies and the grandest of long-summer flower borders into an exotic display in a way that no other plant can. They are sultry and vibrant individuals, some varieties being old, but there are many excellent recently bred ones – they scream carnival and will party hard until winter truly bites. Plant these tender perennials from April for flowers from mid-June until November.

By mid-July, they will flower at their peak like a mixed-species flock of resplendent, plumed male birds of paradise and they will do so profusely on into November. A misty, early autumn dawn is when they are to be seen at their most exquisite and beautiful, with their wet petals to be found misted over, turning their flowers into marooned sea creatures after the tide has gone out.

Dahlias, like tulips, come in many different classes. The ones that I love and grow are classed as 'decorative', 'balls', 'singles' and 'anemones'. The latter two groups are packed full of nectar and flower late in the year at a time when a profusion of flowers is hard for bees to find. Such garden-grown blooms provide a lifesaving last supper before bees and some species of butterfly hibernate or migrate for the approaching winter.

The single group include dahlias that are known as Bishops, which have beautiful dark-green, almost black, foliage too. I grow members of the decorative group sparingly. I'll scatter them through their single-flowering, seemingly distant, cousins or amongst airy cosmos, like huge exclamation marks. A demand for them as wedding flowers across the pond in America has seen this group become very much in vogue of late, with more and more of their Ascot-hat-material flower heads appearing. Their downfall is that they are easily damaged by a wet summer and are beloved of earwigs, who will ruin them overnight – the flowers are also totally useless for bees, due to such a profusion of petals.

I tend to grow just a handful of the ball dahlias. They can be tricky for me to truly adore, but they succeed the others in terms of their lifespan as a cut flower, so I grow them for this reason alone.

Clockwise from top left:
Dahlia 'Bishop of Canterbury'. Dahlia 'Totally Tangerine'.

Dahlia 'Labyrinth'. Dahlia 'Bishop of Auckland'.

Dahlias are half-hardy perennials and all of them love the sun. They grow from tubers that look like past their best-before date sweet potatoes, but once they touch moist soil, roots are sent out and growth tips will soon spur to the surface of the 3-litre pot of compost that they should be placed in by mid March, either on a windowsill or in the greenhouse. By the middle of May, the dahlias will be desperate to continue their growth in the ground or in the largest of garden containers that you have.

Once they have been planted outside, their stems must be staked to protect them from the wind. Either tie their stems to canes or encircle them with birch, but normally by June it is in full leaf and therefore useless, so try and cut enough of it down in the winter with some left aside for dahlia staking later in the year.

The dahlia tubers can cope with a degree of cold, but a combination of this and wet weather will see their tubers rot away to mush over the winter. In the south, they can be mulched with a large bucket of compost tipped over the soil they are growing in, once their foliage has been cut down. The foliage of dahlias will be blackened by the first winter frost. The compost will act as a blanket for the tuber under the soil and means they can be left in the ground to successfully reappear in early summer.

In the north, however, leaving them in the ground sees them awaken far more slowly than if they are started off inside. Because of this, I lift all the dahlias in early November. They are labelled and packed into totes surrounded with dry, spent compost. All are then taken up into the greenhouse, where they sleep, protected, until March when I sort through them all and replant each tuber into a pot for its new growing season. With so many dahlias to lift and put to bed, it's a task that easily takes a week, if not longer, but one that is worthwhile for a plant that gives so much to a space. Another advantage to starting them off in the spring like this, rather than leaving them in the ground, is that their new growth tips are protected from slugs.

In containers, dahlias will need to be fed over the summer with a liquid feed such as seaweed or with soaked chicken-manure pellets. To maximise their flowering, feed them every fortnight and water them well weekly. This will see them flower into October. After Halloween, I lift the tubers from the garden. This act sees the garden's last bits of colour evaporate within hours, and the feeling of the year closing truly dawns.

Clockwise from top left:
Dahlia 'Bishop of Llandaff'.

Dahlia 'Chick a Dee'.

Dahlia 'Darkarin'.

Dahlia 'Downham Royal'.

151

Clockwise from above:
Dahlia 'Happy Single Date'.
Dahlia 'Hot Cakes'
Dahlia 'Mambo'.
Dahlia 'Darkarin'.

Clockwise from above left:
Dahlia 'Roxy'.
Dahlia 'Soulman'.
Dahlia 'New Baby' (ball dahlia), 'Bishop of Llandaff' and 'Bishop of Auckland'.
Dahlia 'Hot Cakes'.

Foliage Profile: Fennel

Fennel provides feathered foliage from April then gives tall umbel flowers from July. Sow from seed in April. Its foliage in the spring is a healthy froth, looking especially beautiful with tulips. The bronze fennel is my favourite, planted with parrot tulips and it then continues on to back up Oriental poppies and roses. At dawn in midsummer, the fennel's feather-like foliage will have gathered hundreds of raindrops upon its fronds, shimmering like crystals.

If you're fearful of fennel becoming too liberal in its self-seeding, chop it right back to its base in early June.

Foliage Profile: Red Millet and *Panicum* 'Frosted Explosion'

While I can take or leave the reliant perennial grasses, in the main – aside from my favourite, the golden oat grass with seeding rods that reach 10ft tall easily – I couldn't be without the addition of annual seed-grown grasses in the garden and vase each summer. These smaller grasses will bring a beautiful candelabra-like show to the garden from late June to October.

Red millet is beautiful once it begins to seed, like a child's handheld sparkler, but the real firework display comes with 'Frosted Explosion'. They'll also become natural bird feeders by the autumn, and if you pick them before winter you can dry their seed heads in time to use in Christmas wreathes to beautiful effect.

Foliage Profile: Sweetcorn

Their strap-like jungle foliage is an aid to the late-summer garden – plant them in groups, as they are pollinated by the wind. The varieties that I grow produce cobs for decoration rather than ones to be eaten. I grow one known as 'strawberry corn' for its burnt orange little cobs. These dry beautifully, and apparently it makes superb popcorn too.

Harvest the cobs before the worst of the autumn weather sets in so they don't rot.

Stipa gigantea seed rods in the evening sun, acting like fountains.

May Checklist

Lift gone-over tulips now, as they will need to be cleared from pots to make way for the planting of summer displays. Lift the bulbs with their foliage attached and snap off their seed heads. If these are left on, they will take a huge amount of energy from the bulb – this applies to tulips left out in the border too. Some varieties are worth keeping for next year and will flower well if their foliage is allowed to brown off. Spread them out in a tray or replant them all in a large pot in the corner of the garden to be forgotten about until the autumn. Once they are rediscovered and emptied out of the pot, keep only the fattest bulbs for planting again in the coming winter.

Alliums will begin to take over from the tulips now, but by the time they are in flower, their foliage will be looking tatty. You can cut their browning leaves right back without harming next year's flower. If you cut alliums for the vase, add a splash of bleach to the water so that the onion sap doesn't spoil the water and smell.

Tackle aphids on roses by rubbing wet wipes over affected buds and stems.

Annual flowers can now be planted out in their final positions safely, without risk of being killed by a late frost in most parts of the country. Allow week-old ducklings to happily clear beds of any slugs before planting summer annuals out en masse, or if you are without such help, ensure that you have watered in the organic, natural slug and snail nematode control.

Pinch out the growth tips of cosmos and sunflowers to create bushy plants.

Add trios of comet goldfish to still-surfaced container ponds to stop them becoming mosquito nurseries! If it is a new pond, wait several weeks for the water to balance in its chemistry before introducing fish.

Plant up containers for summer, thinking of the Sarah Raven rules of an eye-catching filler – a draping over the container's rim spiller and a firework-like horizon. Enrich the container's soil before planting with well-rotted manure and blood, fish and bone meal (especially if planting hungry container plants such as dahlias).

Ducks longing to rummage through a wheelbarrow of cleared spring bedding.

May

Plant Profile: Sunflower

The truest living form of antidepressant can be found in bright, flowering sunflowers growing in the garden. Planted at large as a group, they become a flowering herd of swaying giraffe-like giants. When you see giraffes on their own or in pairs licking at branches with their blue tongues at the zoo they, like sunflowers, never look as magnificent or content as when they are in a fuller grouping.

Don't grow the traditional tall dinnerplate sunflowers, though (what really is the point of them?). Although their huge heads, once gone to seed, are a feast for birds – and for your hens if hung upside down for pecking –

the sunflowers that are really worth growing are those that have a branching form. This horizontal branching is encouraged greatly by pinching out the growth tips of seedlings, when the young plants are about 10in tall. This makes the young plants produce side shoots from each of their leaf joints, instead of naturally carrying on upwards and producing one or two large flowers. The pinching-out treatment is like creating a sunflower bush, rather than a ropey, tall sunflower tree. These branching varieties of sunflowers will flower in the garden for several months. As the blooms fade or are cut, more will open.

Clockwise from top left: Sunflowers come in many different colours and sizes thanks to recent breeding efforts; all are meccas for pollinators. 'Sonja' (*top left*) is one of the best for cutting and is shorter than many. The taller in height 'Valentine' and the branching light lemon-coloured 'Vanilla Ice' are also good for cut flowers; these both fill an Emma Bridgewater blue hen sponged jug (*top right*). 'Claret' (*bottom right*) is the richest and truest in colour form of the many-titled rouge sunflower group. The most striking and beautiful with a large flower head, despite its shorter height, is 'Ms Mars' (*bottom left*), which looks incredibly striking in a container.

Wallflowers of the 'Sunset' series planted with the peony tulip 'Antraciet', with billowing bronze fennel and emerging alliums in April.

Summer

The flowering of the foxgloves in the factory garden marks the passing of spring, but it is when the alliums appear that I know summer has truly arrived. With the coming and going of Chelsea Flower Show, and the busy but fun hours helping Sarah, I often return to the factory garden to see the eggs hatching into chicks. As the new arrivals enjoy the sunshine, adult hens will spend longer and longer obsessing with whatever eggs have been laid in their nesting boxes (even by another bird!) and they require being checked on regularly for dreaded mites. Neighbours may suddenly complain of cockerels' crows that can often be heard as early as 4 a.m. – though to my ears it is a beautiful sound.

As the heat rises in the garden, watering everything becomes a daily requirement, and I find myself staking things as quickly as they grow to ensure that the summer storms are not too destructive. The greenhouse empties but is soon filled up again with late sowings of sunflowers and then, in late June, the second spring begins with the sowing of biennials and the taking of tender cuttings. When you live above the shop, or indeed run one, you're always stacking shelves or, in the garden's case, planting beds and pots.

Cider with Rosie – alliums 'Violet Beauty' and *christophii* amongst self-seeded Shirley poppies, whose appearance is ensured by not over-mulching the flower beds.

June Checklist

The dahlias will now need to be staked as they begin to flower and become heavy with blooms. If you're growing decorative types, then place terracotta pots crammed with straw on top of canes close to them. Then each morning empty the straw out into the chicken run. This will keep earwigs, which will otherwise destroy dahlia flowers, in good check as they will gather themselves in the upside-down pots. It's also excellent enrichment for your hens.

Stake quick-growing plants such as sunflowers and cosmos.

Dry, browning allium heads can be kept for Christmas displays. Hang them upside down inside, so they may dry and lose their seeds without causing a mess.

Deadhead or, better still, pick annuals that will now be in bloom. Sweet peas especially need to be picked every few days – including their tendrils, as these take away energy from flowering. If you're going away, then invite a friend around to do the task for you, with the cut flowers being the most lavish reward for them taking the time to do this helpful deed.

Cut back herbs such as rosemary and sage if they seem to be woody, with lots of top growth but bare bases. Some of the fresh top growth can be taken as cuttings.

Cut back the foliage of Oriental poppies hard to the ground, once their flowering has finished.

Add washed, shop-bought bags of watercress to container ponds to help deter green water. Skim the water's surface with a net for invasive floating duckweed, then feed as a beloved treat to your ducks.

Hens that begin to moult their feathers may need a diet that is richer than normal to produce new, shiny plumage, so soak their layers' pellets in cod liver oil. You can also further supplement their diet with cat biscuits for extra protein.

Alliums that have gone to seed are picked to be dried for Christmas.

June

Plant Profile: Wallflower

BIENNIAL – SOW IN JUNE FOR FLOWERS THE FOLLOWING APRIL OR MAY

Wallflowers are the modest escorts of tulips – both bloom together, but the wallflowers will continue to do so for several long weeks after the tulips have faded. If you can, growing wallflowers yourself from seed will result in the bushiest and healthiest plants, compared to the often weak and yellowing twigs of those planted as bare-root plants. You can have success with bare-root wallflowers, but only if you plant them early in September. They will then have a decent month of being in warm soil, giving them a chance of growing their roots before it turns cold. However, you'll be limited in choice as to the wallflower varieties that you'll be able to buy in bare-rooted bunches.

The 'Persian Carpet' mix is the traditional favourite. These should bloom in a mixture of rich shades, containing all the feather colours of an old English game cockerel – oranges, deep crimsons and purples – but alas, quite often the mix turns out to be mainly a disappointing rich butter yellow. The new 'Sunset' series looks set to outdo many of the more traditional favourites, however, having a refreshing vigour and zest and appearing healthy in its looks.

Wallflowers will be pecked to sticks by hens within moments – you cannot mix the two together. In some areas, they have become a favourite snack of urbanising wood pigeons too, so they may need some protection from stems of twiggy silver birch.

Foliage Profile: Purple Spurflower (Plectranthus purpuratus)

TENDER PERENNIAL – SUMMER FOLIAGE

A true rainforest plant, but one that is surprisingly giving in the garden, providing lush, frost tender foliage to a summer container. Buy in an adult plant, then take cuttings to increase stock in midsummer. They are very easy to grow from cuttings, so if space and time allows, do this each June and treat them as annuals. Overwinter the young plants in the greenhouse or on a windowsill, rather than saving the huge parent plants from the frost. If you have the space, these can become conservatory plants too, as it seems a little wicked to just allow the frost to turn them to mush. Saved from the frost or not, their rooted youngsters will grow with speed come the spring and reach the same size as the original parent plants by late autumn.

'Persian Carpet' wallflower with tortoiseshell butterfly.

Below left: Wallflower 'Blood Red'.

Below right: Wallflower 'Giant Pink'.

Plant Profile: Poppy (Papaver)

Poppies are one of the most divine yet fleeting flowers within the garden, with their petals seemingly cut from the deepest, finest, crinkled tissue paper.

Most self-seed themselves over midsummer and then flower between May and June. In order for a garden to be full of annual, free-spirited poppies, they must be allowed to self-seed. Your eyes must then learn to tell the tiny seedlings apart from other garden weeds when they begin to germinate in spring. Deep mulches and careless actions with a garden hoe will see them disappear from a garden.

Opium poppy (Papaver somniferum)

A lavish, ball-gowned beauty with its foliage and flower buds being duck-egg blue in colour and mostly smooth to the touch. The flowers last around two days, then their petals fall to reveal the most perfect of seed pods which extend the garden use of this plant. Once dried, the seed pods are good to be saved for Christmas, when they can be sprayed golden or bunched together in their natural colours in a vase.

Opium poppy varieties include 'Black Beauty', 'Cherry Glow' and 'Dark Plum'. All will interbreed, resulting in semi-doubles, doubles and singles, ranging from wishy-washy pinks and lilacs to sultry reds and deep clarets.

Oriental poppy (Papaver orientale)

More willing to be tamed and more reliable in their garden appearances are the perennial Oriental poppies. In full flower, they are the closest thing to having a flock of flamingos standing one-legged in the garden, should you be brave enough to flock a number of the same variety of Oriental poppies together. The Orientals flower in May, so buy in adult plants of specific varieties then divide them once they have flowered in June.

Once they have dropped their last petals like feathers to the ground, take the hedging sheers and chop the whole clump right back hard to its base. The hairy green foliage will then begin to return within the month, albeit more modestly, and the plants will cope with then being shaded out for the rest of summer so you can plant annuals like cosmos around them.

The perennial Oriental poppy 'Patty's Plum' was the first plant that I ever bought from Chelsea Flower Show. It possesses petals of the deepest, most delicious blackcurrant sorbet colour. This varies a little, it seems, between strains so buy it in flower to ensure that you have the most sultry specimen.

Oriental poppy 'Patty's Plum' paired with ornamental thistle (*Cirsium rivulare*).

July and August **Checklist**

Use seaweed and chicken manure-based feeds fortnightly for container plants to maximise flower production and help ensure that foliage remains healthy and green. Tomato feed is also of use.

Sweet peas will begin to turn now and go to seed by the end of the month, with their flowers getting so short that they can't be arranged unless a whole tendril is cut. Once you have arranged the last vase of them, chop them down and plant/train into their places the later-flowering climbing annuals such as *Thunbergia*.

Sow biennial foxgloves from seed in July.

If not already done, sow wallflowers and decorative winter vegetables such as kale and chard.

Cut dahlias, sunflowers, cosmos and other summer flowers for the house weekly, from now into October.

Deadhead waterlilies and remove dying lily pads.

Be on guard against hungry vixens with cubs to feed, making them bolder than ever in both urban and rural locations to dine on easily poached poultry.

Hang the heads of seeding sunflowers up for the hens to peck at, or leave out in the garden for finches and sparrows to enjoy.

Deter stubborn, unwanted broody hens from their sitting by blocking off nesting boxes. If this fails, put them in a wire dog crate with a bare, wired base along with food and water. Place them in this sin-bin existence, somewhere open but still secure and sheltered from the weather, for (if you can bear it) two weeks, then let them back out. This treatment will make all but the most stubborn of hens break from their sitting.

Curly kale is to an extent resistant to cabbage white butterflies and to most well-fed buff Cochin hens. Ensure you rotate where you grow your kales to prevent cabbage root fly.

July and August

Plant Profile: Foxglove (Digitalis)

BIENNIAL – SOW IN JULY FOR FLOWERS THE FOLLOWING MAY TO JUNE

Foxgloves are towers of nectar and are the best flower to show children how the process of pollination occurs, as masses of big bumblebees are to be seen buzzing up and down their tubular blooms all day long. Sometimes, the solitary bees fall asleep within them and also use them as shelter from the rain.

Place packets of their seed in the freezer's top drawer a month before you sow them in early summer to ensure that the seeds then germinate quickly.

If you pick foxgloves when they come into flower in late May to early June, this can help to ensure a longer flowering season, albeit the flowers that grow after the main stem has been cut won't be as tall as the original king one. If your garden is to their liking, and if you leave their stems standing to dry and go to seed, then foxgloves will self-sow themselves willingly, but often they cross-pollinate themselves back to their original deep pink, rather than the cultivated peach, purple and white bred varieties.

As is always mentioned by people when they are seen in a vase, foxgloves are poisonous – but only if they are eaten!

Foliage Profile: Caper Spurge (Euphorbia lathyris)

BIENNIAL – SOW IN JULY FOR FLOWERS THE FOLLOWING JULY

This is my favourite euphorbia, perhaps surprisingly, as most people don't know much about it. This may be due to it being considered a wild weed by many. I grow it for its June flowering. Everything about caper spurge screams reptile to me! When it flowers it will reach 2m high and the unnoticeable flowers will then fade to reveal little green pumpkin-like seed pods. These I collect in July and dry, sowing them in August. They grow quickly, making little lizard-like seedlings. They are a biennial, so they need to be sown each year. I have yet to see them for sale as seed, so if you spy a seeding plant in a friend's garden, ask for some seed to take home so you can then grow your own.

Like all euphorbias, if you cut them, their milky sap can cause skin irritation.

Right: Foxglove 'Suttons Apricot'.

Far right: Caper spurge.

Late tulip 'Victoria's Secret', crimson broad bean, caper spurge and Gladiolus communis subsp. byzantinus.

173

Foliage Profile: Kale (Brassica oleracea) and Chard (Beta vulgaris)

Both edible vegetables give invaluable foliage through the winter and then add to the displays of spring hyacinths and tulips in the spring. I sow their seeds under cover in August with the wallflowers so that they can be planted together on top of bulbs, mostly in containers or lining the paths in rows. From an early August sowing, they will be large enough to survive the winter.

I hate anything in the garden that has to be covered with netting in order to save it from either pigeons or caterpillars. The curly kales seem to resist the latter, thankfully. After the spring show you can leave chard and kale in place. In the case of kale 'Redbor', its purple coral-like leaves look beautiful with almost anything, and chard, when it's allowed to become tall and wild in its habit of going to seed, looks like some sort of crazed octopus, and the seeding stems can look beautiful when picked and placed in a vase on their own.

On a winter's day, the sight of rainbow chard (*Beta vulgaris subsp. cicla var. Flavescens*) with its vivid yellow, pink and red veins will not fail to give you some cheer and you'll be glad to have grown it just for this.

Dwarf kale and hyacinth 'Anastasia'. Hyacinths can be effectively used to greet March with clout before the tulips flower by combining them with muscari and crocus as the final top layer of a bulb lasagne. Hyacinths of the richest colours include 'Woodstock', 'Jan Boss', 'Peter Stuyvesant' and 'Dark Dimension'.

Foxglove 'Suttons Apricot', alliums, fennel and cornflower 'Black Ball' in early June.

Autumn

As autumn creeps in, the dahlias reach their peak and the garden dances into chaos: an overfilled cup of Venetian colours framed like stained glass. At this time of year, on a sunny morning, I always feel the air is worth getting up early for to be immersed in. Young pullets need sorting from their brothers, and I have to decide which debutants are to be kept for next year's flock and which are to be put up for sale to make room for new young birds. All too soon, the wallflowers are crying to be planted out and, with a heavy heart, the dahlia jungle has to be cleared bit by bit to allow these and others to get their roots down while the soil is still warm, the hessian netting saving them from the pecking of the hens.

Bulb catalogues arrive, immediately rousing thoughts of spring to help distract me from the chill that is setting in. Pumpkins mark the garden's seasonal closing – dotted around, placed on bales, stuck onto thick upright branches, they provide a comical half-term trial for visiting children and adults alike, and the hens enjoy pecking out their insides of mushy pulp and seeds. After Halloween the garden's door closes to visitors and I start to prepare for the winter months.

Dahlia 'Mels Marmalade' with pumpkins laid out for Halloween before the garden closes to visitors for the winter.

September **Checklist**

If not grown from seed at home, plant wallflowers in their bought bare-root form while the soil is still warm. If this is not possible, due to lack of space in the garden as a result of late-summer-flowering annuals, then pot up the bare-root plants so that they can form a proper root ball. This will give them the best chance of surviving the winter, and looking half-decently green through it, too.

Plant out all other biennials in the garden now, if space permits. If it doesn't, ensure that they are well fed in their pots until you can plant them out. If their root balls are congested upon planting them, tear their bases with your fingers to encourage them to root into the ground quickly.

This is also the best time of year to plant newly bought perennials and shrubs. The soil being warm and wet will see them establish quickly.

Now is the best time to buy new hens, with breeders having a good selection of young pullets and breeding trios (one cock and two hens). Slowly mix young pullets with adult hens over several weeks to avoid bullying by the older, established birds. Another hen house and run may often be required to begin with. Dust all new birds directly with a mite powder.

Worm all your hens now, both newly bought and resident, with a medicated feed containing the poultry wormer 'Flubenvet' for a period of one week. This should be done twice a year – in late summer and early spring.

Mix dahlias with blackberries and spindle berry from the hedgerows for the vase.

Hedgerow harvest.

September

Plant Profile: Blue or Purple Tansy (Phacelia tanacetifolia)

HARDY ANNUALS – SOW IN SEPTEMBER FOR FLOWERS IN APRIL/MAY THE FOLLOWING YEAR (OR MARCH OR JUNE FOR FLOWERS IN THE SAME YEAR)

This is a plant that can be scattered direct as seed onto the ground without the fuss of seed trays, pricking out and hardening off, and are marvels for those who are short on time or growing space. They are useful to both the novice and experienced gardener alike.

Phacelia tanacetifolia is one of the most showy and beautiful seeds to be treated in this independent manner. It has yet to be given the limelight that it deserves as a garden flower, as it is still largely seen as a green manure to be dug in before it flowers to improve the production of a vegetable bed – hence its seed packets will normally be found in the vegetable seed racks. If you let it flower, however, the scent of wisteria and the sound of bees will fill the garden as its lilac flowers begin to bloom. Its delicate form is of a healthy green foliage that is covered with fine hairs, and from this will arise its flowering stems. At first, they are colourless green fuzzballs, but gradually they darken to purple before opening to reveal a beautiful lilac flower that is unlike any other; there is something beautifully mystical about it.

It can be sown in the autumn in September, or even as late as November if it's still mild and the location is sunny. This will result in it flowering with wallflowers and tulips the following year. Otherwise, it can be sown in mid-spring – make sure that the ground it's being sown into has been dug over and raked to a fine consistency.

(Another annual and unusual blue flower that is a half-hardy, but well worth growing, is the beautiful, ruffled flower of the shoo-fly plant (*Nicandra physalodes*). Following the flowers come its seed pods, which are like Chinese lanterns.)

Opposite top: Phacelia with tulip 'Blue Parrot', having been sown in the autumn on top of the planted bulbs.

Right: Phacelia and bee.

Far right: Phacelia.

Hydrangeas, picked just before the hard frosts come but when the first cold mornings ensure that they ripen to a beautiful blueberry smoothie of purple and blue; these I allow to naturally dry in the vase, with sprigs of panicum 'Frosted Explosion'.

October and November **Checklist**

Order autumn bulb catalogues, selecting your favourite varieties of tulips straight away to avoid disappointment. The most in-vogue ones will sell out fast from premium suppliers.

Pick heads of hydrangea to dry, as now they will be at their most lavish colours before they turn brown.

Collect dry, faded artichoke and cardoon heads from the garden, spraying them silver and gold for Christmas.

With a heavy heart, clear the garden down fully, removing the last annuals before they become a mushy mess – the frosts won't be far away.

Mulch dahlias with several inches of compost if they are to be left in the ground over the winter. Otherwise, lift each clump on a dry day. Label each tuber as you do so, as once the flowers and foliage have gone each tuber looks the same. If they are at all wet when lifting, dust them with yellow sulphur to help deter fungus and rot. Place your labelled and sorted tubers into dry plastic boxes full of compost, in a frost-free and airy place.

Lift summer gladioli corms too, and lily bulbs if your soil is heavy – they may rot if left in soggy, cold soil.

Plant tulips by the hundred between now and Christmas, layering them within pots and scattering them through the flower beds.

Plant alliums, narcissi and other spring-flowering bulbs.

Allow the hens to help you clear the flower beds, and then house them in covered-over runs or securely floored greenhouses/poly tunnels so they are sheltered from the worse of the winter wet, wind and cold. Such housing will comply with government regulations should there be a bird flu outbreak over the winter. In such cases, poultry will be required to be kept indoors. Now is the time to start feeding more mixed corn, as the birds will need more energy to keep themselves warm during winter.

October

Plant Profile: Early Spring Bulbs

PLANT OCTOBER TO NOVEMBER FOR FLOWERS IN MARCH

It is worth thinking about a few flowering bulbs for early spring before the tulips bloom. Such bulbs are much cheaper to buy than tulips, too! The exception to the cheap rule is that of the large hyacinths, but these give out a beautiful fragrance. My favourite is 'Woodstock' (*Hyacinthus orientalis*), which has flowers of a beetroot-puree purple. In their first year, these fat bulbs will produce a dense mop head of flowers in March. I like them more in their second season of flowering and in the years after, as the flowers then become less dense and more reminiscent of their bluebell woodland relatives. While those forced for Christmas inside can be grown with just the base of the bulb touching the soil, hyacinths that are set outside in the autumn must be planted several inches below the soil's surface to protect them against frosts.

The grape hyacinths (*Muscari*) are brilliant for little terracotta pots and are very trustworthy for making reappearances each spring. They will behave themselves when in pots, whereas if they are planted in the open ground they will form a dense matt as they multiply.

I previously didn't like narcissi. This was for two reasons – the amount of time they take to die after flowering and the fact that, while they are in bloom, the weather is bound to almost always be cold. There are some elegant ones, though, with rich scents, and my favourite is 'Geranium', which has several flowers to each very tall stem. They bloom late enough to clash with the early flowering tulips, but I don't like to mix them together much, as their forms compete rather than complement each other. I cut the foliage down after they have finished flowering in May, when it is still green, and they still flower come the following spring.

Hyacinth 'Woodstock'
with muscari at Mill Yard.

Few plants could cope growing in small terracotta pots over the summer due to their inability to hold water and a lack of space for root growth. The answer for the auricular stands summer show is a grouping of the tender, drought resistant succulents *Echeveria elegans*, which are happy with minimal attention provided they are in a sunny position.

Muscari in an auricular stand flowering in March.

Plant Profile: Perennial Alliums

People are often surprised to be told that the allium is, in fact, an onion! The game is easily given away, however, if you accidently dig a bulb up from damp earth or slice one in half with a spade – easily done – you'll soon smell a strong odour more familiar to the frying pan than the flower border.

While the tulip gets all the major attention in the autumn bulb catalogues, the allium proves its worth in several ways, most notably in its perennial habit and its flowering time, filling the lull of the dreaded May gap. Alliums are also a favourite bloom of the bumblebee. Once the flowers have faded in July, take them inside and dry their heads as they make beautiful Christmas decorations.

If your garden is to be filled with tulips, then it's a good idea to place one allium bulb for every five tulip bulbs when planting them in the autumn, so that you don't just have a decaying mass of gone-over tulips – an especially important factor to give consideration when planting a small garden. This way, as the tulips fade the garden will be festooned with purple glitter balls.

To do well, alliums require a soil of good drainage, like most bulbs, and they do like the sun too. If your soil is heavy with a large amount of clay, add handfuls of sharp grit mixed with spent compost to their planting hole so that they don't become soggy and rotten during the winter.

The strappy, smooth leaves will appear early in the year. They become a bit shabby by the time the flowering stems have risen up from their centres, but at this stage you can cut the leaves off without harming next year's display. Given the mentioned conditions, alliums will last in the garden for decades, with their display multiplying each year. This habit results in them being cheap bulbs to purchase, compared to tulips.

Clockwise from top left:
A sadly rare visit to the garden from a migratory Painted Lady butterfly, feeding from the allium 'Violet Beauty'.

The upturned jellyfish-like Allium schubertii.

The last and smallest allium to flower is the July flowering *Allium sphaerocephalon*.

Nectaroscordum siculum – known as Bulgarian honey garlic, this member of the allium family has flowers like a chandelier, which the bees will dance under, and it thrives in shade.

191

Alliums ensure that the garden's show does not dip in excitement once the tulips have totally faded out.

November

Plant Profile: Tulip (Tulipa)

PLANT BULBS NOVEMBER/DECEMBER FOR FLOWERS THE FOLLOWING APRIL TO MAY

The thought of next year's displays of tulips will see me through the winter months, even on the darkest and dullest days. I will have planted hundreds, if not thousands, of their ripe, fat conker-brown bulbs, often into late December (planting them at this time helps to reduce fungal diseases like tulip fire), so I know that the result will be the most vibrant, vivid flowering display of the garden's year. The beauty of them is that, once they are planted, that's the work done, provided they are healthy bulbs in the first instance and the soil they have been planted into drains well – you then just have to wait for spring to see them come into bloom.

New tulip varieties are bred in Holland each year so, like dahlias, the ones named here may be out of fashion by the time that this book is printed! The expense of tulip bulbs reflects their size, quality and how newly bred the variety in question is. This is because of the time it takes to grow a crop of tulip bulbs (several decades, in fact) to the point of harvesting them for retail sale.

For the best visual display, just select around four different varieties, several of a similar shade then one to act as a gate crasher to the rest. You'll want to plant at least fifty of each type, or a hundred if expense allows, to ensure a huge impact come the spring. Think about early, mid- and late-flowering varieties too, so that you have tulips in the garden from April until late May. Increasingly tulips are being bred with scent in mind, as they can have a very similar scent to that of freesias.

Some tulip bulbs, the parrots and flamboyant peony types, are often best treated as spring one-hit wonders. These large and brassy tulips take so much energy from the bulb that they are pretty much spent after their first flowering outing. This isn't always the case if they are planted deeply in the garden, rather than in pots, and if their foliage is allowed to brown and crisp off after flowering. Snap off their seed heads after their petals have fallen. They may then come back for another few seasons, but the most perennial in habit are the classic-looking varieties – the 'Viridifloras' and 'Darwins'. These are most likely to provide several seasons of blooms.

I treat tulip bulbs planted in pots in the same way as bedding bulbs and then I'll discard most of them when I lift them up in June to make way for the summer bedding. Normally, the heat of them growing in a pot will cause the mother bulb to wither as it puts its energy into growing baby bulbs from its base.

Clockwise from top left:

Tulip 'Dolls Minuet'. Tulip 'Request'.

Tulip 'Orange Favourite'. Tulip 'Chato'.

195

A bulb lasagne

I plant tulips into dustbins, troughs and large pots in layers of three, one on top of the other, a technique that Sarah brought back with her from Holland, known as a 'bulb lasagne'. The method allows a pot to be crammed full of around thirty bulbs. The first layer of bulbs is planted at about 15in deep, then compost is put on top of them and the second layer of bulbs is planted. This is repeated, and the top layer of bulbs is finally planted with a layer of compost to the top of the pot. The bottom two layers of bulbs simply grow around the bulbs above them when their growing tips hit their bases.

Tulips are best planted into fresh compost and they must have good drainage to thrive, or they may rot. Ensure that this is the case in pots by placing gravel and broken terracotta or bits of polystyrene in their bases before planting them with bulbs, and if you have heavy soils, mix in grit and spent compost when planting them into the ground. The grey squirrel is a huge bulb thief and pots may need to be protected with chicken wire and a sprinkling of chilli powder or flakes in areas where this non-native tree rat is at large!

Clockwise from top left:
Tulip 'Brazil' – like a golden ball.
Tulip 'Orange Princess'.
A queen tulip bulb.

Tulip 'Ronaldo' backed with bronze fennel.
Tulip 'Blue Parrot'.
Tulip 'Rococo'.

Plant Profile: Roses (Rosa)

HARDY FLOWERING SHRUB – PLANT IN EARLY WINTER FOR FLOWERS THE FOLLOWING JUNE–SEPTEMBER

Pairing just one precious homegrown rose with other blooms such as dahlias or sweet peas takes a garden posy into a different level of decadence, with which only a garden-grown peony can possibly compete. Plant bare-root in early winter for flowers from June to September, depending on the variety.

Gallic/French Rose (Rosa gallica)

It was only after seeing Sarah's enclosed and enchanting rose garden at Perch Hill in early summer that I truly longed for lots of roses in the garden. Here, roses bloomed amongst smoky clouds of fennel. I hadn't seen roses grown amongst and adding to such an abundant, lush scene before. The sight was a far cry from the traditional Victorian rose garden. With other plants complementing and backing up the roses, they were suddenly more gorgeous and lavish to me than ever before.

Roses are cheapest if bought as bare-root plants and planted straight into the ground on a frost-free winter's day. You'll easily pay double the amount of money for the same rose in a pot, and often the soil around its roots falls away as soon as it is taken out to be planted anyway! Order a trio of the same variety and plant them close together for the best visual effect.

Roses like heavy, rich soils and are greedy plants that will thrive on well-rotted hen-house muck. The heavy flowering but often thin-stemmed David Austins will need a good nest of thick birch twigs and bended hazel to help support them during summer storms. The rose staking and training in the garden of Sissinghurst, where many beautiful, rich burgundy types were maintained by its creator Vita Sackville-West is the most meticulous to be seen in the world.

Clockwise from top left:
Rose 'William Shakespeare'.

Rose 'Summer Song' – it should be called 'Caribbean flamingo', due to its flowers being the exact same orange-pink as their feathers. Silver birch has been used as a natural support here.

Rose 'Munstead Wood', which is very fast growing.

Rose 'Tuscany'.

Rose 'Lady of Shallot' in Sarah's Colour Cutting garden at Chelsea in 2017.

The old rose 'Tuscany' is like a velvet sofa of dense rouge with the most excitable yellow anthers peeking through the mass of petals, with good disease resistance too.

Rose 'Darcy Bussell'.

Rose 'Graham Thomas'.

Rose 'Hot Chocolate'.

Rose 'Duchess of Cornwall'.

Rose 'Charles de Mills'.

Rose 'William Lobb'.

Garden becoming jungle.

Winter

Like a reluctant broody hen, one must leave one's nest each dark morning. What does a gardener do in winter? Tulips are planted long into December, layer upon layer of them into troughs, bins and the front of flower beds. The garden is cleared properly – a wax jacket is now badly required – and the space is made as neat as it can be with all of its skeleton showing. This is a season of tidying and cleaning in the tool shed and greenhouse. Roses are pruned and more are set as bare root plants, their purchase in this form being far cheaper than when buying them in a pot!

The shop is decorated for Christmas, allium heads are sprayed gold, peacock feathers are festooned about the place and wreathe-making is taught to people who are attending classes. Like a wood pigeon making a nest, I'll gather leafless silver birch saplings by the bundle load to make next year's plant supports and tepees (though some days I feel I'd rather not get out of bed and bypass winter all together!). The spring seed and dahlia tuber order is listed and, on days too cold and wet to do anything outside, I'll help Zoe with cafe and shop jobs of all varieties.

The hens enjoy the spa that is the greenhouse, with its dry earth that they love to dust bath in out of the cold and wet. Sowing the sweet pea seeds in December and watching the hens fluff up their feathers from the neighbouring greenhouse is one of my greatest winter pleasures.

The garden in winter after a sharp frost. With it being at its back-to-its-bones stage, the hens are in the greenhouse enjoying a spa-like existence.

December Checklist

Aim to have all spring-flowering bulbs planted by the middle of the month.

Think about flowering bulbs that can be brought into the house for placing on the kitchen table for the months of February and March, perhaps by planting iris and snowdrop bulbs in small terracotta pots by your back door.

Deck the halls with the dried seed heads of saved alliums, spraying them gold and silver. Do this outside on a dry, calm day. Spread newspaper out on an outdoor table, then lie the allium heads onto it and twirl them, spraying the paint continuously until they have been fully coated. Leave to dry outside for a few hours. Pineapples also look fabulous with the same treatment!

Sow sweet peas into long pots or root trainers undercover. This will give them time to grow a good, long root structure, which will make for far hardier flowering plants that will resist mildew – much more so than if they are sown in the spring.

Sweet peas 'Barry Dare',
'Lord Nelson' and 'Black
Knight'.

December

Plant Profile: Sweet Peas (Lathyrus odoratus)

HARDY ANNUAL – SOW IN DECEMBER FOR FLOWERS FROM JUNE TO AUGUST

The scent of a bunch of late-June sweet peas sees them remain ever popular, but to grow them well does require some knowledge. They are, in fact, best sown in December rather than the spring, somewhere cool – the windowsill of an unheated room or an empty greenhouse. In the case of the latter location, beware of mice who will treat freshly germinated pea tips as their Christmas chocolates! The reason for this early winter sowing is so that the seedlings can grow a large root run that will be able to support a huge plant, which will then flower its socks off in the summer.

Sweet peas like to be grown in a deep pot, so choose a long plastic pot – the sort that you buy a rose in is good. Four seeds can share a pot such as this, with one seed being pushed into each corner to the depth of the first knuckle of your finger. Seeds can also be sown individually into plastic root trainers, which are very useful. These are the modern version of the traditional toilet roll idea, where they are crammed together in an ice cream carton and filled with compost, but unlike toilet rolls root trainers don't go mouldy or rot away so they can be used again and again. What sweet peas don't like is being unduly disturbed, so it's good if you can sow them into a pot and disturb them just the once, when they are to be planted out finally into the garden.

Some people soak the seeds of sweet peas before they are sown but, while this will speed up their germination, it's not necessary. Without being soaked, the seeds will germinate in about three weeks' time. Keep the seedlings cool so that they don't grow into long, useless whips and, once they have four pairs of leaves, pinch out their growing tips so that they bulk up into hunky little plants. By April, these winter-sown seedlings will be strong and can be planted out, normally by the first week of this month – they will be able to stand any light frosts that may still occur. You can sow sweet peas in the spring, but these plants will be weaker than those sown in the winter.

Sweet pea tendrils are very touch sensitive; they are happiest with birch branches to climb up rather than a slippery bamboo cane, but hessian or jute netting is a good climbing frame for them too. Sweet peas are very hungry plants and will excel when the soil that they are growing in has been enriched with manure. In addition, they will stay healthy and green into late July with weekly feeds of comfrey. Comfrey leaves can be soaked in a bucket and, several weeks later, the leaves will have disintegrated into a foul-smelling brown soup which is highly nutritious for many garden plants. Dilute it with water in a watering can and the sweet peas will grow tall and lush.

Once the sweet pea flowers begin to bloom you must pick them all each week, otherwise they will go to seed and the plants will feel that their work is done and begin to yellow and die. When you pick the flowers, remove their tendrils too – a long task, but these take energy away from the production of flowers if they are left to grow. Sweet pea flowers last around three days when cut, but their scent and colours are lavish, making all the effort worthwhile. Despite your best efforts, by August they will want to be cut down to the ground as they will be looking tired. This is when later-flowering climbing annuals are such an aid in stopping the garden becoming bare.

The 'Spencer' sweet peas are good, with longer stems and large flowers, but for maximum scent it's the oldest types that are the ones to grow, although these often have smaller flowers and shorter stems. Recent breeding efforts have seen these two groups of sweet peas crossbred to try and get the best of both worlds.

The perennial, hardy everlasting sweet pea (*Lathyrus latifolius*) is beautiful too and will come back each year with none of the annual fuss. Alas, however, it has hardly any perfume to be smelt at all!

Above left: Sweet pea 'Black Knight'.

Above right: Sweet pea 'Barry Dare'.

Crocks in trough awaiting compost.

January and February **Checklist**

Organise your plant pots. Clean them in hot, soapy water outside on a decently (rare for this time of year) dry day, to help rid them of fungal spores and to ensure that none are harbouring any slugs on their insides!

Wash the greenhouse glass (if you have one) to ensure maximum light allowance.

Find a plastic tray that fits the whole of a windowsill, if this is going to be the location of your seedling nursery, to avoid unwanted damp when watering and to maximise the space that round saucers under pots will otherwise take up.

Sow sweet pea seeds now, if you've not done so in December. Sow them in pairs in long plastic pots and allow them to germinate inside on the windowsill, which will take around two weeks. Once they are a few inches tall, put them into a cold greenhouse or sheltered porch so that they don't become tall and leggy.

Prune roses. Always do this using washed secateurs, cleaning them between attending each plant, and clear up any fallen leaves around them to reduce the chances of diseases such as blackspot.

Pick stems of dogwood, willow, birch and the black berries to be found upon past-flowered ivy. Shiny Portuguese laurel (*Prunus lusitanica*) and silver eucalyptus (*Eucalyptus cinerea*) arranged cascading and filling a large vase may not need any flowers added to them, but they and the other mentioned foliage will make shop-bought alstroemeria and other flown-in flowers from the supermarket look suddenly lavish and far more beautiful at a time when none can be picked from the garden.

Gather natural material for plant staking, arches and tee-pees now while silver birch and hazel are still in full dormancy or, if you cannot gather these yourself, track down a supplier that you can buy them from by the bundle. Think about the amount of staking that your garden plants will need, considering tall perennials, climbers and heavy summer flowers like dahlias – you'll almost always need more than you think!

Clear any remaining leaves from garden borders as the spring bulbs begin to peek up through the soil's surface.

Order annual and biennial seeds, summer-flowering bulbs and dahlia tubers from mail-order suppliers.

January

Plant Profile: Butterfly Bush (Buddleja davidii)

HARDY SHRUB – PRUNE IN JANUARY FOR FLOWERS IN JULY

The butterfly bush is a plant with the reputation of being a thug. It is a shrub that sows itself and spreads like wildfire on derelict land and along railway tracks up and down the country. People are fearful of its ability to grow, from seemingly nothing, up from cracks in paving and from the mortar around brickwork. Despite its ability to conquer vast areas, the buddleia is not native – it was introduced from China in the 1890s.

Like most plants, if given attention, the buddleia can be a garden-worthy plant and a magnet for attracting butterflies. The key factor is that they need seasonal winter pruning, and this can be carried out from November to February. This pruning is some of the harshest to be done to anything ornamental, and while some gardeners will be less rash with a handheld saw, I am not. A mature buddleia can take being cut right back each year, leaving just 10in of the main woody stem above the ground. As soon as spring takes over from winter, the stump will sprout many shoots that will quickly become tall and arching. The reason for such harsh pruning is because these shrubs flower at their best when spurred on to bloom on fresh growth, so the long tassel flowers will be bigger and better.

It is the flowers that are the main draw of the plant. On the wastelands around Stoke, the buddleias are all mongrels. Reigning supreme is the normal lilac, which is pretty enough, but some cross-pollinated jewels of royal blue and magenta are to be found too, while white ones in full bloom remind me of white peacocks displaying, with their tail feathers fanned out, swaying in mid-air. I pick the honey-scented flowers for events, namely the summer Emma Bridgewater Collectors Club days. They only look good for three days at a push, but for a one-day event or a party they are brilliant crammed together en masse in a vase, although their sap will stain the water brown! Strip all the leaves from the stems, as these flop quickly once they have been cut and seared.

Foraged buddleia.

Me, picking buddleia.

Epilogue

When I began writing this book, I saw it as a record of the garden at the Emma Bridgewater Factory and as a way of getting more people to realise that the factory had a garden at all in the first place. In fact, to do this all I really wanted was a few postcards. To visitors, both new and old, and to all those who know the garden, I hope it is indeed just that, I also hope that it will encourage readers (whether they have a huge long, sprawling garden or just a window box) to grow some of the plants I've mentioned – and perhaps even consider the keeping of hens if space and time allows. After all, I think we all need a few more beautiful flowers and cheerful chickens in our lives, in both ceramic and living form.

Arthur Parkinson, 2018

Hens helping with autumn clearing.

Recommended Suppliers

For all the seeds, bulbs, roses and seedlings mentioned in this book, visit sarahraven.com to receive a catalogue (telephone 0345 092 0283).

For perennials and shrubs local to the Stoke-on-Trent area – T. Derek Thursfield, Kerry Hill Nurseries, visit tdthursfield.co.uk (telephone 01782 302498).

For mail-order English roses and sweet peas as cut flowers, visit realflowers.co.uk (telephone 020 7349 8638).

For coppiced hazel suppliers throughout the UK, visit coppiced-products.co.uk (telephone 01952 432769) or make contact with your local wildlife trust.

For galvanised troughs, visit iae.co.uk (telephone 01782 339320).

For poultry sundries, feeders, health products and feed, visit sprcentre.com (telephone 01243 542815).

For rare and pure-breed poultry, plus hatching eggs, see advertisements in the monthly *Country Smallholding* and *Practical Poultry* magazines. Chatsworth farmyard, Derbyshire, often has young hens for sale towards the end of the summer.

For Pekin Bantams and Pekin Bantam hatching eggs – Bury Green Poultry, Hertfordshire, visit burygreenpoultry.co.uk.

For a breeder of pure-breed pullets – Warwickshire Chicken Coop, Banbury (telephone 07960 693724).

More Resources

Bridgewater, Emma, *Pattern & the Secrets of Lasting Design* (Hodder & Stoughton, 2016).

Devonshire, Deborah, Dowager Duchess, *Round About Chatsworth* (Frances Lincoln, 2005).

Raven, Sarah, *The Bold and Brilliant Garden* (Frances Lincoln, 2001).

Raven, Sarah, *Grow Your Own Cut Flowers* (BBC Books, 2002).

Roberts, Victoria, *Poultry at Home* (DVD, Old Pond Publishing, 2006).

Roberts, Victoria, *Poultry for Anyone* (Whittet Books, 1998).

Arthur Parkinson's gardening and poultry photography may be viewed via his Instagram account @Arthurparkinson_

Emma Bridgewater Factory walled garden in Stoke-on-Trent, Staffordshire. The factory is open all year round, while the garden is open from mid March until October. emmabridgewaterfactory.co.uk

Acknowledgements

This book, or the photographs for it at least, began about three years ago – the blink of an eye in the life of a garden. My residence as the pottery gardener has been almost as brief, but a lot has been achieved within that time. This book is a token of this. Without Matthew Rice's original imagination in creating a garden at the factory, there would be no garden and no need for a gardener. He laid out the garden's bones and planted its fruit trees. Both he and Emma Bridgewater have been very gracious in letting me have total free-range in the garden's planting and the use of their brand in the writing and make-up of this book – long may they both continue to design pottery that renders both fowl and flower on ceramics so beautifully. It has always been lovely to find Emma sat on her great bench when she visits the factory, soaking up the sun, with always a kind, wise or encouraging compliment which, at times, has been much needed. Thanks also to Bubble (Lucy Catling and Rosa Banbury).

Martin Brezina, Emma and Matthew's gardener at their farm in Bampton, is one of the most hard-working people that I have met and excels at the art of vegetable growing.

Before Emma Bridgewater, if it wasn't for me visiting Perch Hill and being taken under the wing of Sarah Raven and her husband Adam Nicolson, who helped hugely with getting the book's form on the right track, I doubt very much that I would be writing this book today to tell such a seemingly rosy tale. They have treated me with kindness and generosity as if I was one of their own children and we are dear friends.

I would like to thank Rosie and Molly Nicolson and the whole team at Perch Hill, who have become like second family – Tessa, Josie, Col, Cally, Mary and Josh.

Jonathan Buckley, Sarah's photographer, has been hugely inspirational, through looking at his incredibly beautiful work over the years.

Day-to-day life at the factory is made wonderful by a number of dear colleagues. I must give mention to Zoe Burrows, Pauline Birchall and Amanda

Past midsummer, an August dawn in the courtyard. Cosmos 'Click Cranberries', 'Rubenza' and the biennial hollyhock 'Blackcurrant Whirl' with grasses and nepeta.

Malley. Pauline brightens up even the greyest of days with wit and intelligent comment, and her opinions on the garden are invaluable to me. We have made many good decisions on what should be placed where together – she's also a very good waterer of the greenhouse. Zoe is the most beautiful and exotic of flowers, whose company I would never want to be without. Amanda is a ray of blonde sunshine, like a canary. Dave West and his team have become experts in building raised flower beds! Thanks to Marion and Amelia in the office, to the gorgeous Jo Blagg, to tour guides Jill, Jane, Rosetta and Elizabeth, to Diane in the shop, and to Janice and Ryan in the cafe. Thanks also to Michael Gajda for always saying good morning in the most upbeat manner without fail; to factory girls Vanessa, Ellie and Jo; and to Graham Bolton for coping with it all!

Thanks to Annie Clark for the gift of a rare mandarin mug, and to Bev Dewhurst.

The photographer Bridget Flemming was hugely kind in sending me several photos of Deborah Devonshire to use. I would like to thank His Grace the 12th Duke of Devonshire and also huge thanks to Helen Marchant and Alan

Above left: Mrs Zoe Burrows.

Above: Pauline Birchall, my biggest support, with Christopher during a photoshoot.

Shimwell, Elaine Oliver of the Cochin Club, the team at Chatsworth farmyard and to Becky Crowley, queen of the cutting garden at Chatsworth.

Juliet Nicolson, my dear friend who I met on a day forever imprinted on my memory – bubbly, kind, wise and warm, and always at the end of the phone with advice and the best of voices.

Thanks to Vicki Allen, who is now mother hen to various fowl that began life at the factory, including Hilary, the Appleyard duck!

Thanks to Mark Wakeling, fellow *Good Life* dreamer, who will one day have his own hens so he can trust the eggs he's eating; to Christopher Spitzmiller (my beloved Buff Cochin cockerel's namesake); to Paul Rose, king of flamingos; and to Caroline and Paul Wright – just absolutely fabulous.

Many thanks to farmer Julian Goodwin for the troughs.

Thanks to Tracy Bailey at Newstead Abbey for looking after the peacocks!

Thank you to Joanna Lumley for taking the time to read and review this book. Joanna (my ultimate tonic) was introduced to me as a youngster – voice first, and years before the sight of her as Patsy Stone in *Absolutely Fabulous*. She was playing the narrative character of an animated orange and black-flecked tiger lily in a televised version of *Alice in Wonderland*, 'In most gardens the flower beds are too soft, so the flowers are always asleep'.

My mum and dad, Jill Parkinson and Nicholas Brown, I thank for putting up with everything and for a pricelessly eccentric early childhood. My grandmothers, Sheila Parkinson and Minnie Florence Brown, I thank for being pillars of wisdom, laughter, fascinating memories and strength. My Auntie Rosalyn Brown, thank you for always believing in me, and thank you Auntie Rosita for all the New Year's Day Chatsworth walks. Great Aunt Iris, my thanks for speaking the truth.

Little Lyndon (Boo), my brother, thank you for always being the one to make me properly smile just by existing. Thank you also to my marvellous and rosy-faced Uncle Chris.

To everyone who has visited the garden and praised it, thank you.

Lastly, to all who have helped with the book at The History Press and to Lindsey Newns for giving this book a chance.

Summer begins.